Swythamley
and Its Neighbourhood

THIS BOOK

was originally printed in London in 1874 in an edition said to have consisted of only 50 copies. This new edition had been entirely reset in Times 11 point by Christine Pemberton and has a new introduction by George Longden. The edition is limited to 500 numbered copies.

This is copy no 158

© The Silk Press Ltd 1998

ISBN 1 902685 01 6

Printed & Bound by Redwood Books, Trowbridge, Wiltshire BA14 8RN

Acknowledgments

The publishers would like to thank the following for their help in the preparation of this book:

Sally Laithwaite of Mereside Books in Macclesfield for the long loan of a rare copy of the original book.

Christine Chester for her generosity in providing original source material.

Joe Longden for making the map of the area described in the book.

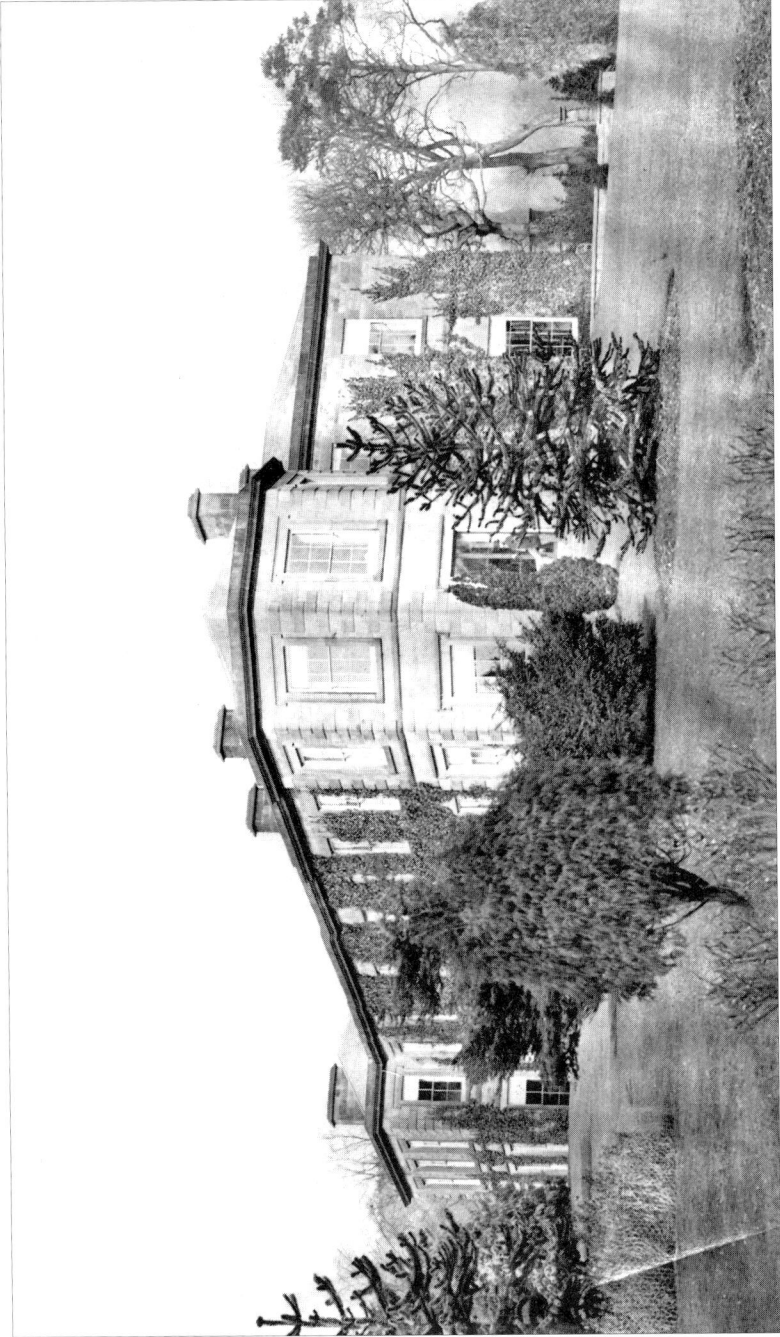

Swythamley Hall

SWYTHAMLEY

AND

ITS NEIGHBOURHOOD

PAST AND PRESENT

Desultory fragments collected from various Authors.

ב פ ל ב

by

Philip Lancaster Brocklehurst

The Silk Press
1998

SWYTHAMLEY AND ITS NEIGHBOURHOOD
Introduction to the Silk Press edition

The originally anonymous author of this privately printed and circulated book was Philip Lancaster Brocklehurst (later Sir Philip), 'squire' of the ancient, remote and beautiful estate of Swythamley on the northern border of Staffordshire.

Philip's family was not long-established gentry. In the seventeenth century the Brocklehursts had been prosperous yeomen farmers, living at Kettleshulme in the east Cheshire hills. The family's fortune was made in Macclesfield in the industrial revolution. Philip's father, John Brocklehurst, was a partner in the firm of J and T Brocklehurst, one of the largest silk manufacturing firms in the country. John Brocklehurst was a Member of Parliament for Macclesfield from 1832 to 1868. Philip's uncle, William Brocklehurst, was manager of the Brocklehurst bank.

It was William Brocklehurst who bought Swythamley Hall and estate in 1831 from the Trafford family who had held it since the sixteenth century. Philip Brocklehurst was adopted by his uncle, and when William died in 1859, childless and predeceased by his wife, Philip, at the age of twenty-one, inherited the estate and the hall which was to be his home until his death in 1904.

Philip at once immersed himself in the administration of the estate, to which he added farm after farm, improving many of them. He was said to be a just landlord. His tenantry prospered, and seem to have been grateful. At the annual rent day gathering at the hall in 1876, for instance, the tenants presented Brocklehurst with a silver collar for a favourite mastiff, and thanked him "for the many benefits we enjoy through your praiseworthy effort in establishing a daily Post, Money Order Office, and Savings Bank in this district. Placed as we are so remote from a town, we feel it a great boon to have our letters brought to us. Many of us remember the time, before you came to reside here, when our letters had to remain a week in the town, till some farmer returning from market could bring them, probably too late to be of service. We are indebted to you for the great improvement made in our public roads, which at one time were so dangerous to travel. We desire also to thank you for the pleasure and privilege you give us of assembling together on so many pleasant occasions in this fine room, our Divine services held here, the concerts and tea parties we are permitted to hold, our monthly penny readings which afford us so much enjoyment in the winter months."

Philip Brocklehurst loved the Swythamley estate and the surrounding countryside for its rugged beauty and for the hunting shooting and fishing opportunities which it offered.

'Swythamley and its Neighbourhood' is a labour of love; the sporting sections in particular, are written from the heart. Brocklehurst, who had been privately educated and did not attend a university, appears not to have had another book in him; if he had, his subsequent marriage and three children perhaps deflected him.

Much of the history, lore and customs of Swythamley and its neighbourhood Brocklehurst took from earlier writers, as he acknowledges with his over-modest sub-title - 'Desultory Fragments from Various Authors'. Considerable use was made of the writings of the youthful William Beresford, published in 'The Reliquary' between 1863 and 1866 as "Notes on a Portion of the Northern Borders of Staffordshire". Some relevant extracts from the parts of Beresford's articles which were not used by Brocklehurst have now been included as an appendix to this edition, providing a wider perspective on the neighbourhood of Swythamley.

The Beresfords were an old Peak family. William was born in Bosley in 1844, the son of Samuel Beresford, Esq. In 1858, he became the first pupil teacher at St Luke's National Schools, Leek (where the pupils included some middle class boys taking subjects such as Latin and Algebra). Beresford attended Lichfield Theological College between 1865 and 1867. In 1882 he returned to Leek as vicar of St Luke's, and later became Rural Dean. He continued to write church and local history, and became a prominent Staffordshire antiquarian.

William Beresford's love of the Staffordshire Moorlands and borders was as great as that of Philip Lancaster Brocklehurst. As a young man, Beresford applied his reknowned vigour to the discovery at first hand of the traditions and customs of the hills and moorlands. His task was eased by the kindness and empathy which later characterised his ministry and made him a popular vicar. The nature of the man was encapsulated in the unsolicited testimony of a Leek farmer (quoted in Beresford's obituary in 1922): "I was at school with him. Not a boy among us could point a finger at Willie Beresford." While Brocklehurst's contact with working people was probably confined for the most part to his tenantry, Beresford talked to small farmers, colliers, button makers and carriers, and in his articles for The Reliquary he described their homes, occupations and beliefs.

'Swythamley and its Neighbourhood' was originally printed and bound with a hundred blank pages interspersed among the text, to which illustrations could be glued. It seems likely that these intended illustrations were photographs taken by or for Philip Brocklehurst. The photographs in the few surviving copies differ in number, and to some degree in content. This edition contains the photographs found in a copy of the book which originally belonged to J D Sainter (author of 'Scientific Rambles Around Macclesfield', 1878) and later to Walter Smith (author of 'Over the Hills Near Macclesfield', 1921, and many newspaper articles on local history), together with some additional contemporary photographs.

CONTENTS

9

Wincle, and relics of ancient times

Whitelee and Gig Hall; the history of Wincle Grange, a paper read in 1853;
Barleighford; the Bridestones; Clulow Cross; Cross-o'-th'-Moor; the two
ladies of Bagstones and their antiquarian treasures; discovery of sepulchral
urn by Mr Sainter, 1871; relics of battles between Romans and Britons;
probable Roman encampment at Wincle; death of a poacher in Otter's Pool,
1868; otters and polecats nearly extinct but poaching prevalent; Wincle
church; graveyard robbing; rush bearing; parish clerk buries a 'little 'un';

10

Miscellania

The loss of the 'Swythamley'; a woman with 107 grandchildren, Leekfrith;
visit of steam carriage to Swythamley, 1868; death of Richard Hassall,
sculptor, 1868; improvement of the local roads by Mr Brocklehurst;

Appendix 1

'Notes on a portion of the Northern Borders of Staffordshire' by William
Beresford (extracts from a series of articles published in The Reliquary
between July 1863 and October 1866).

Appendix 2

Appendix 3

LIST OF PLATES

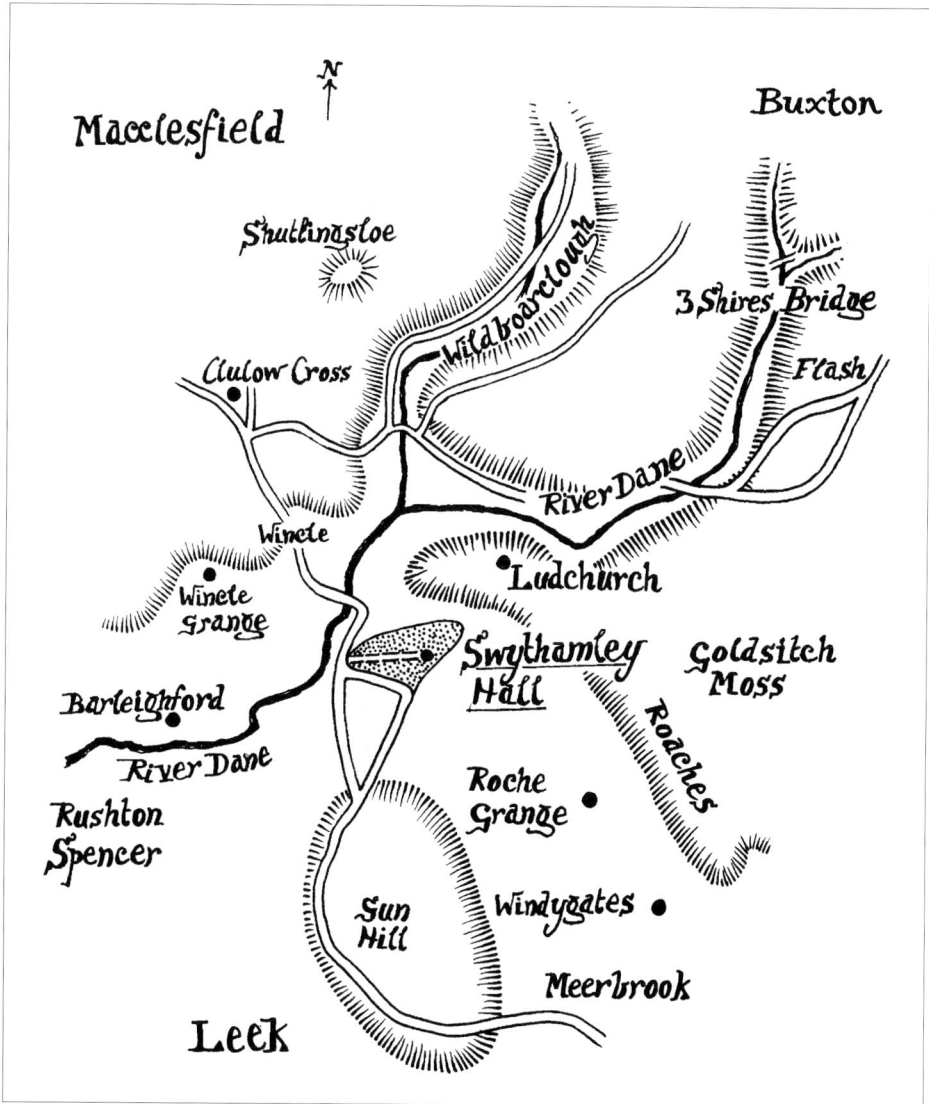

Macclesfield

Buxton

N

Shutlingsloe

Wildboarclough

3 Shires Bridge

Clulow Cross

Flash

River Dane

Wincle

Ludchurch

Wincle Grange

Swythamley Hall

Goldsitch Moss

Barleighford

River Dane

Roaches

Rushton Spencer

Roche Grange

Sun Hill

Windygates

Meerbrook

Leek

Philip Lancaster Brocklehurst

THE HISTORY OF SWYTHAMLEY

Swythamley a mediaeval hunting lodge; foundation of the Abbey of Dieulacres; Dieulacres endowed with Swythamley; the Abbott demises Swythamley to his relative, John Whitney; Swythamley granted to William Trafford by Henry VIII; the Trafford family acquire the ruins of Dieulacres and the manors of Leek, Leekfrith and Rudyard; property sold to Lord Chancellor Macclesfield, 1723; rise and fall of Lord Macclesfield.

SWYTHAMLEY Park and Grange, written in ancient documents Swithomlee and Swythunley, is situated between what formerly constituted the great "chaces," or forests, of Lach and Makelisfeld, and possesses historical facts and legends, intermingled with its history, which denotes it to have been one of those wild and romantically-situated hunting lodges that in the old feudal days existed in the large and secluded tracts of land then untenanted save by deer, wolves and the other feræ naturæ of the country. In Sleigh's "Biography of the Norman Earls Palatine of Cheshire," and in his interesting "History of Leek" (which, with kind permission, is largely quoted in these pages) mention is made that Hugh de Meschines (surnamed Keviliok, alias Boham) fifth Earl of Chester, died at his hunting seat, Swythomlee, A.D. 1180-1, in the forest of Lee, or Leek; and the late Mr Bateman, of Middleton, an author of great authority, considered that the old Danish cross in Leek churchyard was erected to commemorate the Earl's decease in its neighbourhood. Certain it is that a stone has been dug up close to its base, incised with the letters and date "H. Q. C. C. 1180. Hugo, quintus Comes Cestrinæ."

In 1221 Ranulph de Blondeville, sixth Earl of Chester, and Prince of Wales, after his return from the Holy Land, as saith Fabyan, "began to buylde the castellys of Charteley and Bestone; and after he buylded ye Abbey of Delacresse, of the whyte ordre, for charge of cost he toke toll thro' all his lordship of all suche as passyd that wey with chaffre or marchaindyse". This same Ranulph, who from his acts of piety was known as the "good earl," is described by the old chroniclers to have been of dwarfish stature but of great strength and fiery spirit, and distinguished himself not only as a Crusader, but also at the siege of Lincoln, in 1217, when he slew with his own hand the taunting Come de Perche, leader of the Dauphin's forces, in the cathedral, and proclaimed the boy king, Henry III.

The Abbey of Dieulacresse, the ruins of which are about an hour's ride from Swythamley was founded by the Earl being bidden in a dream "to build a monastery of White Monks, where there should be a ladder by which the prayers of angels may ascend and descend." On awaking he tells his Countess the vision, who answering, in French, "Deu encres," he is pleased with the expression and says the name shall be Deulacres - Dieu-la-cres.

The Earl removed thither the Cistertian Monks of his Abbey Pulton in Cheshire, endowing it, among other possessions with his manor and forests of Lach and Swythomlee, together with his heart, there to be buried whenever he should die.

By royal charter (exquisitely engrossed and in the Swythamley collection) dated at Rothelan, 16th December, 1283, Edward I, King of England, Lord of Ireland and Duke of Aquitaine directs his archbishops, bishops, abbots, priors, earls, barons, justices, sheriffs, constables, ministers and all bailiffs to allow his well beloved in Christ the Abbot of Deulacres to have free warren for ever within his demesne lands of Lach (and Swythomlee), yet "provided those lands be not within the limits of our forest of Makeselfeld, so that no one shall enter those lands to hunt within them or take anything which belongs to a warren without the license of the Lord Abbot and his successors, upon

Ruins of Dieulacres Abbey

The Cistercian Abbey of Dieulacres, situated a mile or so north of Leek, was founded in 1214. Its history has been described as turbulent; extensive estates, sheep-farming granges, hunting rights and other privileges brought the Abbot into conflict (sometimes violent) with other landowner, local communities, and the Crown. At the dissolution of the monasteries in 1538 the Abbot and twelve monks, together with a larger number of servants and lay officials, were pensioned off. Most of the stone fabric of the Abbey was probably used in local building; by the 1870s, when this photograph was taken, little remained.

Rushton Chapel

forfeiture of £10. Witnesses: Edmund, our brother, our Chancellor; R., Bishop of Bath and Wells; Gilbert de Clare, Earl of Gloucester and Hertford; William de Bello Campo, Earl of Warwick; Geoffry de Geynville; Eustache de Hacche."

The sporting Abbot, however, was not to be restrained; and, in anticipation of fat haunch and venison pasty, the favourite food of the good old monks, it is recorded he was indicted (Harl. MS mmlxxii, p.7) "for that his houndes took 2 stags in the forest of Makelisfield; which two stags were carried to his abbey of Dieu-la-cres and there received for use." The Lord Abbot pleaded that when the deer were slain he had not been appointed to the abbacy, and that he ought not to be made amenable for his predecessor's poaching.

Considerable mention is made of the Abbey of Dieu-la-cresse in this account of Swythamley, from the fact that, at various periods of their respective history, the relations of the Grange to the Monastery were much intermingled, each having in turn, as it were, possessed the other - ancient records showing that in A.D. 1534, and prior to that date, Swythamley was the residence of John Whitney, to whom it had been demised by his brother or relative, Lord Thomas Whitney, last Abbot of Dieu-la-cresse. In little more than a century after, we find, by deeds and other authority, not only the remains of the Monastery but almost the whole territory between Leek and Swythamley in the possession of the Trafford family, through a marriage with Mercy Rudyerd, of Rudyerd. The estate of Swythamley, measuring about seven miles across, has therefore this peculiarity, that, since the reign of Edward I, nearly six hundred years ago, it has only been in the possession of two families - that of the Traffords and its present proprietor - many of the homesteads bearing the same name as they did then, with some little difference in the mode of spelling.

In the year 1158 was founded the Abbey of Pulham in the County of Chester; this was subsequently translated to Dieu-la-cresse by Ralph,

Canon of Chester.

Among the patent rolls, xxxiv, Henry VI, A.D. 1430, it is shown that "Rudheath," in Cheshire (now the property of John Taylor, Esquire, of Booth Hall, Lancashire), was held by the Monastery of Dieu-la-cresse, and that round the boundary of Rudheath rode Ranulph, Earl of Chester, causing three ploughs to plough after him to define the said boundary. The royal grant and seizin was read before Lord Pagan Tibtolt, justice of Chester.

Extensive and great were the powers and privileges exercised by the Abbot of Dieu-la-cresse and his monks of the white order, since we find enumerated among them those of fure and waif, infangthef and outfangthef exemption from terrene service, talliage, passage, murage and all customs whatever.

Among the Marquis of Westminster's deeds is a lease for forty-nine years, from John, Abbot of Dieulencres to Nicholas Manley, of the Manor of Pulton. Moreover the aforesaid Nicholas agrees that he will give the Abbot and his successors with twelve mounted companions, entertainment for six days, twice a year: wine, fresh salmon and oysters alone excepted. "Dated at Dieulencres in our Chapter House, April 16, 1504."

Mariota, daughter of Hugh Carpenter, A.D. 1268, made a gift to the Abbey of a burgage, and an acre of land in Maxfield (bought of Richard Carter): witnesses, Ad' de Sutton, Rd. de *Falingbroome* and Thoms. de Gostworth.

Roger de Menilwarin also gave to the monks, for the health of his soul and of Ranulph, Earl of Chester and Lincoln (his mother's brother), free common in his wood of Pevere with husbot and haybot as they should have occasion, in the presence of his foresters, and pannage for fifty hogs. (*Dugdale*.)

Several of the old monastery seals are still in a good state of preservation; in the "Reliquary," and in Sleigh's "History of Dieu-la-cresse," a seal is engraved, bearing the Virgin and Child seated beneath a gothic canopy; it is on one of the Abbey deeds in the possession of Mr Brocklehurst, and is also attached to a parchment belonging to Mr Warburton, dated May, 1337 (Coles MS xxvi., 246) containing the deposition of John Whitney, late Chamberleyne to Lord Thomas Whitney, last Abbot of Dieu-la-cresse. Hereby it appeared that four or five days after the suppression of that Abbey, A.D. 1538, "several blanks having the convent-sealle were seene by the deponent, the Abbatt and others be'ng privy." Upon these blanks the Abbot's scribe, Wm. Damport, wrote leases with ante-dates.

On a parchment preserved at Swythamley, bearing the convent seal, Lord Thomas Whytney, the Abbot, demises to his relative and Chamberleyne, John Whitney, then resident and seated at Swythunley, "all ye auncient Graunge and Parke londs of Swythunley, with the titles and Manor of Hayton."

This deed was subsequently cancelled by Sir Thomas Bromley, Knt., Chancellor of England, and Sir Gilbert Gerade, Knt., then Attorney General. "The said Graunge and Parke of Swythunly Manor of Hayton, being at the dissolution of the Abbey seized by Henry VIII, it was granted by that King to 'his dearly beloved William Trafford, of Wymslowe, Esquire, to be holden of us *in capite* by ye service of the 20th part of one knight's fee.' Mem. that this patent was executed and possession was "delyvered and taken in the Manor and Graunge of Swythernley and Heaton the 10th of June following;" these, *inter alios*, being witnesses: Edmund Savage, Esquire, Justice of the Peace, for Chester; Thos. Whytney, late Abbot of the Monastery of Delincresse; Sir Hy. Ryle, Parson of Wylmslow, and John Lee de Rygge. - "And possession was taken in the Hie-foreste of Swythurnley at the howse of the keper of the seid Hie Forest" on the same day. (The Royal Grant, in excellent condition, is with the other records, and has been lithographed).

For some offence it appears that the estate was afterwards confiscated, since we find James I, by deed dated 1623, restoring it to William Trafford after taking his fealty.

Mention is made that previous to the destruction of the Abbey, a magnificent race of great white mastiffs (molossi) were kept by the monks, but, after their dispersion by Henry VIII, the breed of dogs appear to have been lost.

The remains of the Monastery was granted by Edward VI, in 1552, to his "welbelovyd survante, Sir Ralphe Bagenholte, Knight," by whose collateral descendant, Sir Henry Bagnall, it was sold, 1597, to Thomas Rudyard, of Rudyard - an ancient Saxon family settled at Rudyard, four miles from Swythamley, *temp.* Canute the Dane, 1030. - (MSS of Wm. Hadfield, "an antiquarian of no mean repute." He died 1852, and a portion of his MSS for a contemplated history of Staffordshire is now in the British Museum.)

In A.D. 1684 the Abbey ruins, with the Manors of Leek, Leekfrith and Rudyard, with the fairs and markets of Leek, the patronage of Cheddleton and Horton, the rectory and advowson of the Church of Leek (The 26th Vicar, Eden Lea received his presentation from a Trafford) with the mines of coal to the same belonging, came into the possession of Wm. Trafford, Esquire, through his wife Mercy, and her sister Margaret Rudyerd, of Rudyerd. At this period a great tract of country was held by the ancient family seated at Swythamley; but in 1723 a large portion was sold to the Lord Chancellor Macclesfield, Wm. Trafford retaining his Manor of Swythamley and Heaton, and continuing to hold there his *Courts Leet* and *Court Barron* as heretofore, the custom of holding the Courts being preserved until lately by Mr P.L. Brocklehurst, the present Lord of the Manor. The first Lord Chancellor Macclesfield, who possessed himself of Rudyard, was, writes Lord Campbell in his "Lives of the Lord Chancellors," born at Leek, in 1666 (in an old house still remaining, at the top of the

Market Place), and was the third son of Thomas Parker, who carried on the business of an attorney, and by the savings of a long life, accumulated a fortune of nearly £100 of annual rent. He was taught to read by his mother and was sent to finish his schooling at Newport, in Shropshire. Thomas Parker, the son, established himself in Derby, where he prospered beyond his most sanguine hopes. He was made one of the counsel to Queen Anne, and knighted in 1705. In 1715, George I raised him to the Peerage as Baron Parker, of Macclesfield, and in 1718 he became Lord High Chancellor - "a Chancellor," to quote still further from Lord Campbell, "who, instead of 'fetching his life and being from men of Royal liege,' and tracing an illustrious pedigree for a thousand years, was the son of a village lawyer." In consequence of some malpractice, he was impeached by the House of Peers, and in 1725 fined £30,000 and removed from office. His descendants are now flourishing and distinguished in the Peerage of England. Thomas Augustus Wolftenholme Parker, sixth Earl of Macclesfield, is the present Lord of the Manor of Rudyerd.

In 1818, the ground where Dieu-la-cresse Abbey stood was examined, and a plan of the Abbey and buildings was published. Many beautiful bosses, gurgoyles, corbels and a stone coffin with crozier and sword carved thereon was found. Traditions of concealed wealth and subterranean passages still linger about this once secluded and still highly interesting and singularly picturesque locality.

RUSHTON, AND THE TRAFFORD FAMILY

Rushton chapel described; the formerly wild countryside around Rushton; how Drummer's Knob got its name; customs and lore of Rushton; Swythamley mortuary chapel; ancient lineage of the Trafford family; William Trafford escapes Cromwell's soldiers; relics of the civil wars; Prince Charlie stays at Royal Cottage; relics of the rebellion of 1745.

Hugh le Despenser, Earl of Winchester, held Rushton Spencer (which took its name from him), but being attainted of high treason, his lands were forfeited, 3 Edward III. That monarch, 16th July, 1334, granted it to Sir Roger Swinnerton, and Maude Swinnerton, an heiress, brought it, cir. 1400, to her husband, John Savage, of Clifton, knighted at Agincourt, 1415.

A distinction is made between the Manor and Township of Rushton Spencer, in which Rushton Chapel stands, and the Townships of Rushton, James and Heaton; the former being within the Manor of Horton, and the latter itself a Manor, of which must be regarded the Abbots of Dieulacres, who possessed Swythamley for centuries prior to the Reformation, as lords in their day, as the owner of that estate is at this day.

A very interesting description has been written of Rushton Chapel by the Rev T. W. Norwood, M.A., of Cheltenham, and the Rev W. Melland. In this ancient church, dedicated to St Lawrence the Martyr, and built originally almost wholly of timber work, temp. Henry III, thirteenth century, there is what is probably almost unique in England, viz., six dog teeth cut in *oak* over the piers on the north side of the nave. The massive circular stone font is considered coeval with the earlier structure. Over the east window is the date, 1630. The situation of this humble, but highly picturesque little place of worship is eminently striking, perched as it is on the summit of a steep elevation, apart from the village, and screened by noble old black firs and ancient yew trees of enormous size. Tradition has handed down that at one time it was surrounded by dense woods and that a squirrel could hop from tree to tree to Swythamley. Two broken stones, standing on either side the porch, are alleged to be of Druidical origin.

Dog teeth in *stone* are to be found in many old English churches as on the north side of the chancel of Astbury, which chancel aisle is coeval with Rushton Chapel.

In the graveyard of the chapel is a stone with this curious inscription: "Memento Mori. Thomas, son of Thomas and Mary Meaykin, interr'd July 16, 1781, aged 21 years. As a man falleth before wicked men, so fell I. Bia, thanatos." Thomas Meaykin was a Rushton boy; he died at Stone, in Staffordshire, and was buried there. A favourite pony pawed the grave open; the body was then disinterred and was found to have turned over in the coffin. It was removed to Rushton where they laid the corpse with its feet to the west, which is evident from the position and lettering of the headstone. The memory of this story is perpetuated in three languages, and was registered by the parson at the time.

There were two trees standing in Rushton, on one of which was written, "Church Way," and on another, "Earl's Way," which served as waymarks through what *now* is a precarious country enough, but what *then* must in truth have been a "waste and howling wilderness." This is demonstrated if we glance at the following names: in one direction we have *Wolf-low*, in another *Wolf-dale*; then comes *Boars-ley* (now written Bosley), *Stags-hill*, and lastly *Wild Boar Clough*.

Cloud, which rises 1,190 feet above the ocean level, is partly in Rushton Spencer, the view from whose lofty summit is most magnificent, extensive and varied. Leek, Congleton and Macclesfield

Trafford's Tomb

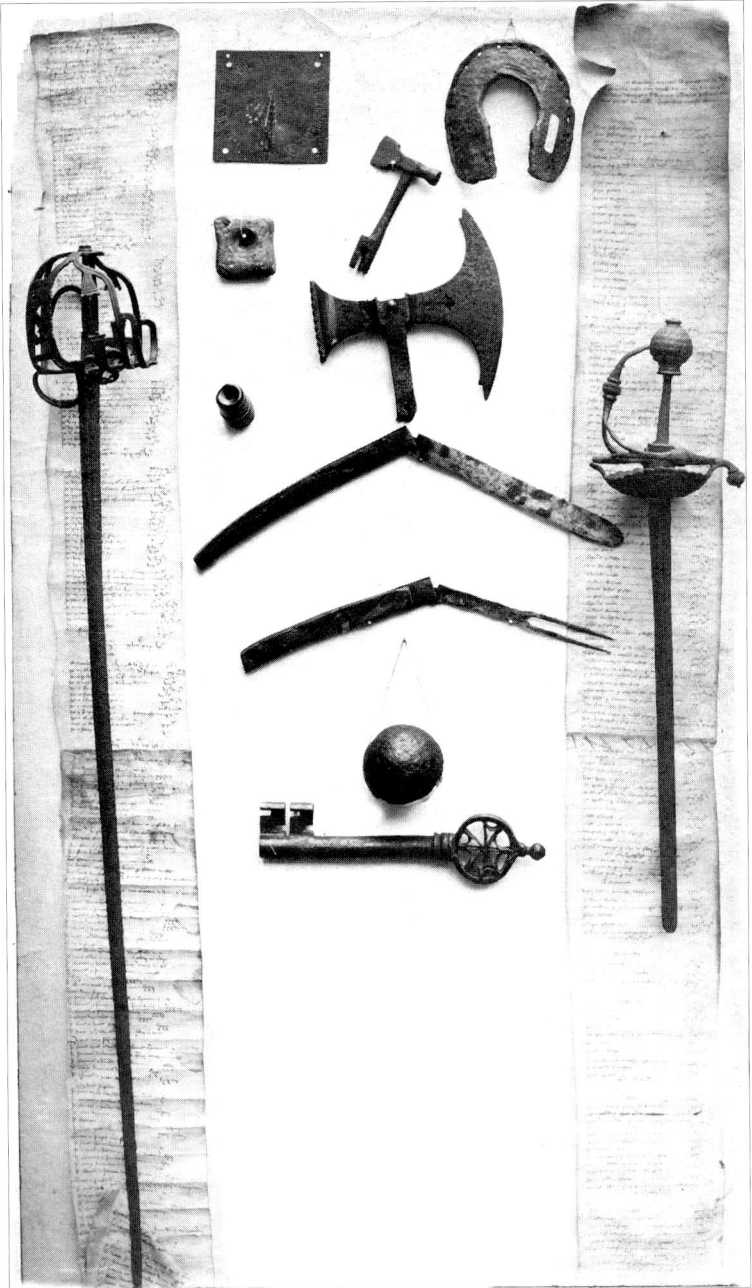

Relics of the Rebellion of 1745

are in sight; Bosley and Rudyard Lakes; the Cheshire and Staffordshire hills, specially the broad Minns, the towering Shutlingslow, Mow Cop, Gun and the Roaches, with a wide range of country interspersed with dale and wood.

The Drummer's Knob, another point of Cloud Range, half-a-mile nearer Leek, and close to the Congleton turnpike road, takes its name from the following incident: - When the Scotch insurgents passed this way in 1745, a drummer sat down and amused, himself singing or playing, "Hie thee, Jamie, hame again." When a soldier asked his officer permission to have a shot at him, the leave was given, and the drummer was killed.

St Daniel's Well is a noted spring near Rushton vicarage, and a notion has long prevailed that it becomes dry on the eve of any great calamity. An ancient custom called the *well dressing* is performed once a year at this spring, which is then prettily decorated with evergreens, and the country people come to dance and make merry, the vicar generally taking an interest in their amusements.

The Romish custom of begging *"soul-cake"* is kept up in this chapelry. On All-souls' Day (November 2) a party of youths call at the farmhouses, repeating the following old but somewhat profane lines: -

> "A soul cake, a soul cake,
> Pray, good dame, a soul cake;
> One for Peter, two for Paul,
> Three for Him who made us all.
> Pray, good dame, a soul cake."

The practice is called "souling."

The following account of St Helen's, or Daniel's Well, is from the *"Compleat History of Staffordshire"*. At page 107 occurs the following:-   "At Rushton Spencer is a well, called St Helen's, which is fed by a spring: yet sometimes it so comes to pass that this well will grow dry after a constant supply of 10 years, all of a sudden, as well in wet as in dry times. The people think that when it so happens there will follow some stupendous calamity of dearth, war, or some other grand revolution. Thus they tell you it grew dry before the civil wars; and again, before the martyrdom of King Chas. I; and again, against the great dearth of corn in 1670; and lastly in 1679, when the Popish plot was discovered. These rustick observations have posed our philosophers."

The quaint little Church of Rushton, called in bygone days the "chappell in the wilthernesse," in Leek parish, belonged in such right to the Abbey of Dieu-la-cresse, but existed long prior to the early foundation of that monastery. Attached to Rushton Church is the Swythamley Mortuary Chapel, the private entrance to which, from the exterior, was discontinued and panelling substituted by Mr P.L. Brocklehurst, who at the same time renovated the interior and restored the old family escutcheon of the Traffords on the chapel ceiling. Underneath is their family vault, and it may not here be out of place to note something of their ancient lineage.

Arms of Trafford: *Or, a griffin* (Loxdale); *a man with a flail, thrashing, saying "Now, thus."*

William, second son of Sir Edward Trafford, of Trafford, Knight, was under-sheriff of Cheshire, 1540, and father, by Margery his wife, of Philip Trafford, seated at Swythunley temp. Elizabeth (ob. 17th July, 1612), who m. Ellen, da. George Dickens, of Sheldon, Esquire; and had William T., of S., who m. Sarah, da. Thomas Homersley, of Cheddleton; and had William T. (buried at Leek), aged 47 at the visitation of 1663, who m. Mary, da. Ralph Bagnall, of Oncote; and had (Philip, second son, who m. Elizabeth, da. Thomas Gresley, and ob., s. p., 1676) William Trafford, of Swythamley (third son, who was buried in the mortuary chapel at Rushton, 26th December, 1726, æt. 82), m. Clara, da. William Lawton; and had William T., of S., (and Edward, maternal ancestor of Trafford Trafford, of Outrington,) who (ob.

October, 1762) m. Sarah, heiress William Stonehewer, of Barleyford, and had four sons, who all ob. s. p.; and a da., Sarah Trafford, of S., who m. William Nicolls, of Stafford. He ob. before his father-in-law, leaving five sons, of whom Thomas N., the eldest, ob. s. p. Edward, second son, m. - and had three sons and four das., and ob. 21st March, 1806. His eldest son, Edward Trafford Nicholls, assumed the name and arms of Trafford, and m., first, Sarah Worsley, of Whitgreave and had Sarah, m. John Joule, of Stone Abbey. He m., second, Mabella Worsley, by whom he had Eleanor, Emily and Julia Anne. He ob. 26th February, 1839, æt. 56, after serving the office of high sheriff in 1818, and selling the manor and estates, August 10th, 1831, to the late William Brocklehurst, of Tytherington Hall, Esquire. (*Hadfield and others.*)

Major-General Thomas Samuel Trafford, youngest son of Edward Nicholls, born at Swythamley, cir. 1786 (ob. 5th January, 1856, after marrying, second, Maria, da. John la Marchant, Esquire, of Melrose, Guernsey), m., first, Anne (ob. July, 1843), da. B. Rawson, Esq., of Bradford Manor and Midd Hall; and had *inter alios*, Charles Guy T., b. 29th January, 1821, who m. Caroline Anne, da. Rev John Hopton, of Canon Frome Court, Herefordshire, and has Edward Guy, Henry Randolph, Lionel James and Clare Ellen.

Near the vicarage house in the burial ground of the old church in Leek is an upright stone, recording the death of William Trafford, Esquire, a distinguished royalist, who died at Swythamley, in 1697, æt. 93, and who saved his life from the fury of a party of Cromwell's Ironsides, by disguising himself as a thrasher at work in the barn. When the soldiers, after ransacking the Hall, found him, he answered their interrogations merely by uttering the words, "Now, thus," between every stroke of his flail, upon which they considered him mad, and departed without further molestation. In this character he is represented on his gravestone, and his family introduced the words, "Now, thus," as the motto on their arms. A rapier of that period was discovered hidden in the cleft of a large and ancient holly tree, that had been blown down by the wind, in the pleasure grounds near the house; Mr Brocklehurst's woodman, while sawing the tree in halves, found his saw impeded by the blade of the sword, which was completely imbedded in wood, the great fork of the tree having through lapse of time grown entirely round the weapon. It is now preserved as a curiosity in remembrance of the visit paid to the old squire by his unwelcome guests. Swythamley has not since been disturbed with unloyal visitors, except in the rebellion of 1745, when the Scottish insurgents, commanded by Charles Edward Stuart and the Dukes of Perth and Athol, passed by on their march to Derby. On that occasion, Prince Charles remained the night at a farmer's cottage, near the confines of the *Back Forest*, giving it the name of the *"Royal Cottage"*, by which it is still distinguished. Foragers were sent forward to Swythamley and relics of their encampment are yet occasionally met with; a Lochabar axe-head inlaid with brass, and an enormous knife and fork of singular construction were presented to Mr Brocklehurst by Mr Robert Hulme, of Heaton, in whose family they had been preserved since the time of their discovery on *Gun Moor* shortly after the passage of the insurgents. A leathern wallet, in a much decayed state, was found at the same time and place.

THE UPPER DANE AND FLASH

Nature at her wildest and fairest in the neighbourhood of Swythamley; the primitive life of the natives; iron working, coal mining and button mould dyeing near Three Shires Bridge; Flash and the Flashmen.

Few English districts are more interesting to those who love to study nature in her wildest and fairest states than the neighbourhood of Swythamley; there the varied scenes of country life are just emerging from their natural simplicity: valleys, rivers, rocks and hills lie mingled in profuse variety; the purple heather blends with the green moss, and toppling crags rise out of verdant woods. Indeed almost every spot has a charm of some peculiar kind, and many of the landscapes are picturesque and beautiful.

A wilder and more thoroughly moorland scene than *Castle Cliff*, a mass of rocks piled up, taking the form that some old Norman keep fallen into ruin might assume, in the midst of the *Back Forest*, near the weird-looking archway into *Lud-church*, could scarcely be imagined. Bold and heath-covered hills, traversed seldom by the foot of a stranger, and perpetually echoing with the murmur of the rock-bound river Dane, abounding -

"With here and there a speckled trout and here and there a willow," and which flows for miles through the deep and shaded dell at its foot, is a place that almost seems to retain the solitude which it must have enjoyed in the earliest years, where the fern owls and hawks rear their young, and the wily fox and cunning badger still prey upon the black game and red grouse.

In upland districts like this, where the means of transit are bad, the soil poor, and the cultivation defective, we generally find the inhabitants leading a primitive sort of life, and somewhat behind their Lowland countrymen in intellectual development and social progress. The mountains among which they dwell seem to divide the current of improvement, and to turn it in two streams by their sides. Thus it is that many of the primitive customs, wild legends and frank simplicity which characterised their fathers, still linger among the present population.

Heaps of half-smelted ironstone, just below the surface of the soil, indicate that this mineral was at some period found in the neighbourhood, and worked there, or was carried from a distance in *panniers* on the backs of mules, for the purpose of utilising the timber for charcoal, which grew in the large forests adjacent. Not far off, near a rock called the *Forge Rock*, was a building for beating the rude metal, also a place for smelting the stone; but they have all, long since, become things of the past.

Pannier's Pool, alongside the ancient mule track, is situated at the junction of Cheshire, Derbyshire and Staffordshire. Crossing over *Pannier's Bridge*, by the brook which enters Dane at the *three shire heads*, you ascend the stream; the water gradually deepening in colour until it changes from a light to a reddish yellow. The mouths of old, disused coal-pits are here met with, and seams of the glossy mineral can be seen cropping out by the brook-side. A little higher is the place where the coloured water runs out of a tunnel made to admit air to the "Penny Hole" Mine and to drain it. The country people call it *alum water*, from its peculiar taste; but analysis proves it to be largely impregnated with peroxide of iron. Its petrifying qualities are so strong that any "small organism" placed in it becomes changed into a stone-like body in twenty-four hours. This spring is probably the same as that described in the *"Compleat History of Staffordshire,"* where is remarked, "Between *Blue-hills* and *Clusterberry-edge*, in the parish of Leek, is a stream as salt as the salt springs in Ingestre Marsh, which tinges the stones all along as it runs, of a rusty colour, and dyes the

Three Shires Head

Flash Village

button-moulds of the Flash button-makers black in half-an-hour's time if made of oak, and with the least infusion of galls, turns as black as ink." Button-making has long since fallen into disuse in this bleak country, and was never carried on to any extent, as the Flash men of those days were not much given to industrial pursuits.

We are now in the vicinity of *Flash*, where years ago dwelt the noted "*Flashmen*.". It is a wild and barren place - heath, stone walls and black commons meet the eye on every side, and there is scarcely a tree to be seen for miles. One stands in a perfect labyrinth of hills, with deep and narrow valleys running in almost every direction. The cottages on these dreary moors are generally as ugly and as low as possible, and seem hugging the ground to avoid the winds. Still you will generally find a white apron, a clean floor, with a bright fire and smiling faces in most of them. Sufficiently near the top of one of these great hills, stands strange little *Flash*. There are in it a number of stone houses, very grim, but built so as to be as cold-tight as possible. In a quiet, modest burial ground is the "Church of the Village"; it is of stone, with a small tower and a nave. Sir Henry Harper gave the half-acre of ground on which it was built in 1744. *Flash notes* and *flash coinage* may possibly derive their signification from this wild, out-of-the-world district, as at one period there was, within a few miles from *Flash*, a noted gang of coiners, known as the "Meg Lane Gang," whose rendezvous was a secluded farmhouse called "Meg Lane Farm." Members of this notorious gang were dispersed amongst the Flash hills and in situations which enabled them to carry on their nefarious trade for a long time with impunity. Fearful robberies and murders were committed, and for a period all the attempts of justice were completely baffled, until at length a clue was obtained from a girl who lived with one of the men at Chester. The farmhouse passed into other hands and has since undergone great alterations; but in clearing out a well in the yard, various implements were found, amongst others a perfect coining machine, worked by a powerful screw for punching out the coin and for striking the impression. This engine is now in the possession of Mr Smith, of Langley, Sutton.

LUDCHURCH

Castors Bridge; description of Ludchurch; snow taken from Ludchurch to Leek market in July; Trafford's Leap; recently reopened cavern; Sir William de Lacy's tale of the Lollard Walter de Lud-auk and the death of his grandaughter Alice.

About two miles westward of Flash lies *Gradbatch*, a scattered hamlet on the banks of the river Dane. A little further down, the hill which at *Quarnford* shuts in the valley on its southern side, opens to allow the *Black Brook*, a clear, pelucid stream, emerging from a densely wooded gorge, the death scene of many a wandering woodcock, to fall into the Dane. A wooden bridge spans the water, and standing on that and looking towards Swythamley, some two miles away, a truly fine scene presents itself.

On the right murmurs the Dane along the foot of a steep and lofty hill sweetly clothed with verdure, and part of Macclesfield Forest; to the left a narrow valley spreads its waving foliage to the sun; whilst in front the *Back Forest*, part of the old *Leek Forest*, full of pine and larch and oak, steeply slopes from a great height to the water's edge. Through this sylvan country its present owner, Mr Brocklehurst, has formed pony paths, that in the spring and autumn afford pleasant rides to lovers of nature. We are now near celebrated ground. This wooden bridge occupies part of the space once filled by *Castor's Bridge* or *Smelter's Bridge* -

> "With its arch of dark grey stone,
> And battlemented sides, by moss o'ergrown."

43

Its romance may be found in the story of the forest, called "Spell Bound," published in 1850 by a Moorlander who had good opportunity of hearing the Forest legends. If, after crossing the bridge from the Gradbatch, or eastern, to the Leek frith, or western side, you look up before you above the woody scene, you will discover a cluster of rocks in the shape of an ancient castle, hence termed *"The Castle Cliffs."* From the bridge to them, and between the Dane and Castor's Bridge, runs the grass-grown remnant of an ancient road. After ascending by it to Castle Cliffs, the tourist should particularly notice a little footpath striking southward out of it, and running along immediately above the plantation. By omitting to do so, many have failed to find a ravine they have come long miles to see. After a short distance, the path suddenly bends into the hillside between two tiny cliffs overshadowed by mountain trees. Passing on, the traveller goes under a low, rocky portal, and then finds himself in a very remarkable place; on every side but one he is beset by rocky walls, having the sky for a canopy. Let him go down the flight of steps which wind away from the more open side, and beyond the curve he will find the place prolonged, but with a stupendous magnificence as imposing as it is unexpected. Before him the uneven path winds away to a considerable distance, rising and falling according to the ground, and widening and narrowing variously between two and seven yards. On either side the rocks rise up in rugged lines, sometimes perpendicularly and sometimes overhangingly, to a height of from fifty to seventy feet. The place is narrowest in its deepest and shallowest parts, viz., at the northern and southern ends. There the tops of either side almost touch each other, but elsewhere they are some yards apart, though never much more than ten. The rocky sides, creviced and apparently tottering like ancient walls; every little chink in them occupied by luxuriant growths of fern; long pendant grass here and there decorating them; hollies, small oaks and mountain ashes bending their graceful foliage from every ledge; the moss, the gorse and the long heath peeping over in rich profusion from the moor above; together with the blue sky, with its fleecy clouds or shining stars for a vaulted roof, give such a natural magnificence and irresistible charm to this grand "Old Temple," as to place *Ludchurch* beyond a parallel in the moor-lands, and to give it a widely-spread and an ever-increasing fame.

The authority of Dr Plott on the Natural History of Staffordshire is so good as to be almost unquestionable. He records that the sides of Ludchurch "so overhang, that snow has been known to remain there through a summer, whereof was signal proof, on Leek fair-day, 27th July, at which time a Wharnford man brought a sack of snow thence, and poured it down at the Market-cross, saying, he could help them to a hundred loads."

Old Squire Trafford of Swythamley, when out with his hounds, once found himself so unexpectedly near the brink of Ludchurch, that, to save his life, he, by voice and spurs, forced his horse to jump the chasm, which was safely accomplished, though several of the hounds were dashed to pieces. The spot still bears the name of *"Trafford's Leap"*. A flight of twenty-four steps leads out of the place at its southern end, but the ravine itself winds on a few yards further, until it terminates in a deep hole, recently reopened by its present owner. From the bottom of this hole the renowned cavern of Ludchurch descends far below, the roof in places being a great height, but as large stones and rocks repeatedly fall, the descent is attended with great risk and danger. There are men still living who have partly explored it and got to where they could distinctly hear the noise of water flowing - possibly the Dane - one of the explorers being William Mills, of the Roche, a man of great courage and veracity. He, provided with ropes, a lantern and a large ball of twine to guide his return journey, was under ground some hours, and thought that there were some signs of Druidical remains, and also steps having the appearance of masonry, but nothing is definitely known about it, as the visit was not repeated. Lord Macaulay, in his essay on "Milton," says that the most uncivilised people are the most *poetical;* and the idea seems to be corroborated by the fact that the older inhabitants of the country around Ludchurch, a wild and unpolished race, had many romantic notions about this cave. Their traditions are to be met with in the works from which these notes have been extracted, but though curious and interesting, they are too voluminous for transcription. One of them which appears to be the most accredited, is as follows, and will be best told in the words of the good knight Sir William de Lacy, who visited the district in the reign of Henry VIII:-

SIR DE LACY'S TALE

It was in the summer of the year 1546 that I, Sir William de Lacy, left the hospitable mansion of my old friend, Trafford of Swythomlee, and turned the head of my gallant steed towards the town of Buckstone. Crossing over a wild tract of country I entered upon a rugged and, in some places, almost impassible path. Sometimes it wound along with dull, jading uniformity; at others it would skirt a lofty range of hills, where the bracing breeze, laden with the perfume of the heather, was wafted from the neighbouring moor. Descending from the hills, it dipped into a lovely valley, so completely enshrouded in trees, that notwithstanding the vivid heat of the sun, a delicious coolness was experienced on entering it. In the centre of the valley, gurgling and rippling with musical glee o'er the sparkling white pebbles, glided a clear limpid stream, the waters of which seemed so cool and refreshing, that I could not refrain from drinking of its crystal drops. O water! how sweet art thou! thought I. The road from this delightful valley skirted for some miles the base of a range of hills. On the right, and several feet below the path which I pursued, rolled the swift waters of the Dane. High, on the other side the river, arose another range of hills, their sides clad with dark heath. The day was extremely beautiful; the golden sun, in his glowing chariot, seemed to drive along heaven's blue vault with fierce, impatient haste, dispersing the white clouds which, a few hours before, hung in graceful drapery about him. Notwithstanding the excessive and almost overpowering heat, I rode along, enjoying the scenic beauties displayed on every side of me. Far in the foreground stood an extensive and dense forest. The sight of this forest, with its waving foliage and dark arched recesses, suggested such an idea of coolness, repose and quiet, as only he, who has been exposed for some time to the heat of a summer sun can fully appreciate. As I drew nearer the forest, and began to experience its delicious coolness, my thoughts, which had been rather disturbed by the great heat, began to assume their usual equanimity, while my mind became more fully alive to the beauty of the landscape.

A narrow but well beaten path wound along through the forest, which in some places was so extremely dense, that all view of the sky was precluded. The forest appeared to be several miles in extent, and abounded in fine and ancient trees. There was the elm, with its rich branches, bending down like clustering grapes; there was the ash, with its smooth bark and elegant leaf; and the silvery beech, and the gracile birch, - the dark fir, affording, with its rough foliage, a contrast to its more beautiful companions, whilst it shot far above their branches with a spirit of freedom worthy a child of the hills. But above all, there was the noble, stately and wide-spread oak, of whose gnarled and iron form Spenser so truthfully remarks - "The builder oak, sole king of forests all." I rode on for a time, sometimes impeded in my progress by overgrown underwood, or by the low branches of some dwarfish tree. At length I approached some comparatively open ground, where on one side the trees were much thinner, and I was then enabled to catch a view of the opposite hills, now bathed in the golden light of the sun. I had scarcely reined in my horse to take a better survey, when I was startled by a loud noise. On turning round, I perceived a rather strange and unusual occurrence. A large and powerful wolf was engaged in desperate combat with a goat. The wolf, with the natural ferocity of his nature, fixed his teeth in the neck of the goat, which, after vain attempts to disengage itself, began to drag him deeper into the forest. Dismounting, I set off in pursuit, to see the issue of this strange combat. The ground was overgrown with heather and low brambles, which much incommoded me, but at length I reached the mouth of a gloomy-looking glen, into which I entered. In breadth, the place was extremely narrow, with damp walls rising to a considerable height; the top was so overgrown with heath that little light could penetrate; consequently a deep gloom pervaded the place. This, and the extreme stillness, impressed me with a feeling of solemn awe. So as soon as my eyes had become a little accustomed to the darkness of the place, I perceived that the goat had been victorious. The wolf lay extended on the ground, gored to death, and the victor, on seeing me, scampered off as fast as possible. As I was returning, I saw, seated at the foot of a lofty oak, which grew near the glen, and whose gnarled and iron trunk had probably witnessed the march of centuries, a neatly-dressed old man, engrossed in the perusal of a worn Bible. He rose, and saluted me as I approached. "This is a very odd-looking cavern," I remarked. "True, my friend," he replied; "but the Almighty, whose power can exalt the humble, and lay low the high, has been pleased to make this cavern, insignificant as it appears, the instrument of many righteous works." At my request we sat down, and the old man related to me the following legend:-

"The immediate followers of Wicklif - the dawning star of the Reformation, as he is called - were denominated Wicklifites, or Lollards. The latter word is by the best authorities, supposed to be derived from the German word *lollen*, signifying to sing aloud, in allusion probably to the extreme fondness of this sect for vocal music. Walter de Lud-auk was one of the most zealous supporters of the Wicklifite doctrines; so that the ecclesiastical authorities sought every

Ludchurch

Old Jim Barber and William Mills, explorers of Ludchurch Cave

opportunity to criminate him. This cave was once much larger than at present, but one of those strong convulsions of nature, which undoubtedly formed the ravine at first, by a second stroke caused it to collapse into its present narrow condition; and perhaps," said the old man, "another stroke may close it for ever. However, Walter de Lud-auk was in the habit of repairing to this cavern during the summer months, with several of his friends, where their devotional exercises might be conducted with safety. Sometimes they made this place their abode, while they spread themselves over the country, extending their doctrines among the peasantry. Many were the searches made for them; but at that time the forest was so large and dense, and the cavern so well concealed, that all search was fruitless. On these occasions the Lollards kept close, while food was conveyed to them by Henrich Montair, the head forester, who was devoted to their interests.

"It was a fine summer afternoon, when the Lollards assembled to perform divine service in the natural cavern of Lud Church. Upon an elevated mound, in the upper part of the church, stood the good old minister. Walter de Lud-auk was about seventy years of age: his hair was bleached like the hoary top of Snowdon, yet his form was erect; and what was still more strange, his broad and massive brow was unclouded with a single wrinkle. Neither his voice nor his intellect had suffered from the iron and relentless hand of Time: the former was strong and melodious, and was equally fitted for vocal praise or pious exhortation; the latter could, with the same ease, grapple with the keen and subtle arguments of the Romish champions. Walter de Lud-auk was a man eminently fitted for the post and faith which he had chosen; his strong mind and indomitable will were well calculated to brave the wrath of the Catholic Church; while his gentleness, exemplary piety and the weight of learning and age, could not fail to make a favourable impression. The assembly, fourteen in number, was ranged in a circle, having their pastor at their head. On his right hand stood a beautiful girl, Alice de Lud-auk, his granddaughter, whose parents, dying when she was an infant, left her to the care of her grandfather, whom she generally accompanied in his journeys. She was about eighteen years of age, rather taller than the generality of women. Her form was light and sylph-like, with a head exquisitely shaped; her brow broad and fair like her grandfather's; indeed, her fine features and graceful form made up a picture of loveliness which the stern old walls of Lud Church rarely viewed. Among the rare qualities with which she was endowed was a matchless voice; indeed all her family were blessed with this enviable gift, but she, like a diamond surrounded by less precious stones, surpassed them all. Separated from the rest of the congregation, and almost at the entrance of the cavern, stood, or rather leaned against the wall, the herculean form of the head forester. Henrich Montair was of gigantic stature and strength; his features were cast in that striking style, called the Roman - large, dark, full eyes, keen as the falcon's; the aquiline nose, and curved and haughty mouth. The expression of his features was rendered still more striking by his bronzed complexion and curling, black beard. He was clad in a coarse dress of Lincoln green; his legs were protected by strong buskins of deer-skin. In his belt was a heavy broad-sword, a huntsman's horn, and a long dagger. At his feet lay a crossbow and a sheaf of arrows. After a short but earnest prayer from the pastor the opening hymn began. How beautiful and solemn did that hymn sound, as every note and every voice rose in strict accordance and harmony with each other! The lofty and sweet tenor, with the deep and musical bass, mingled their dulcet notes together in fervent praise to the Most High. At a certain part of the hymn, the other singers stopped, and the wild, bird-like strains of Alice de Lud-auk warbled with an almost unearthly sound - so remarkable was the compass of her voice - through the vaulted chamber. And when her voice was at the highest pitch, and when all eyes and thoughts were engaged in devotional contemplation, a quick trampling of feet, and a ringing of arms, were heard. Before any movement could be made, a tall and powerful man, clad in steel, rushed in at the entrance, followed by others. The voices of the singers were hushed - the man stopped short, and, waving his sword, cried, "Yield, in the name of the blessed Church, and his most Gracious Majesty King Henry." The Lollards seized their weapons, and prepared to stand on the defensive, but were commanded to desist by their pastor. All obeyed, except the forester, who darted forward, and seizing the officer in his iron grasp, dashed him with such force among his followers, that they were irresistibly borne back to the entrance of the cave; then drawing his sword, he called to the Lollards to escape through the other outlet, while he defended the pass. One of the men levelled his arquebus, and fired, as the forester pressed forward; the bullet whistled past his ear, but a loud shriek burst from behind. The forester turned hastily round, almost afraid to trust his eyes; his foreboding was but too true; he saw the beautiful Alice supported in the arms of her grandfather, - the fatal bullet was lodged in her bosom. Uttering a terrible cry, the forester sprang forward, and flung himself, with the desperation of a wild beast, upon his foes. His great stature and strength, and the narrowness of the pass, were formidable obstacles to the assailants. Two had fallen, cleft to the teeth by the mighty arm of the forester, whilst all shrank from encountering those terrible, death-dealing strokes.

"There was a pause. The men held back; and the giant forester leaned on his bloody sword, his dark eyes flashing fire from beneath his shaggy and lowering brows. A low sound now issued from the violated temple, like the plaintive sighing of the wind; it grew stronger and stronger; till at last the lofty and solemn death-chant of the persecuted Lollards could plainly be heard, swelling in rich, yet mournful strains, as it rolled forth from the cavern and floated on the breeze, then declining in cadences of touching tenderness and melancholy pathos, it ceased - and the songs of the Lollards never more issued from Lud

Church. So solemn and wild was the place, so awful the event which had called forth the beautiful, yet unlooked-for hymn, that even the rough natures of the soldiers were touched, while the strong chest of the forester heaved with emotion. A few moments after the last sounds of the chant had passed away on the wind, Walter de Lud-auk, bearing the fair corpse of his granddaughter, and followed by the Lollards in solemn procession (carrying with them pickaxes and spades), issued from the church. At a few yards from the entrance, the Lollards began to dig the last resting-place of Alice de Lud-auk. The soldiers were grouped around in silence, for there is nothing which makes so great an impression on the mind, as a glimpse at that state through which the perishable matter of all earthly things must pass. The grave was dug, the corpse lowered, and soon the earth covered the lamented remains of her who, one short, fleeting hour before, lived in the possession of youth and beauty. Thus do the temporal things of this world pass away, like morning dew before the mid-day sun. The good old pastor, upon whose countenance grief was strongly depicted, but who, with the Christian fortitude of all good men, bowed in submission to the will of his God, kneeled down and signing to his companions in adversity to do the same, he offered up a short, but fervent prayer. Then rising with a dignity which no misfortune could overcome, he, with his friends (including the forester), peaceably submitted to the soldiers. Little more of this melancholy legend remains to be told. On the way to London, the forester conceived his plan of escape for the whole party, but they refused to profit by it: De Lud-auk, however, aware of Montair's danger, for his imprudent resistance to the officers of justice, ordered him, on pain of his strict displeasure, to convey several papers of importance to France. After considerable resistance, Montair obeyed, made his escape, and embarked for France, where he resided until the invasion of the English, whom he joined. Of De Lud-auk's companions, some were imprisoned for a short time, and the rest pardoned: the fate of De Lud-auk himself was never known, but it is supposed that he died in prison."

After the old man had concluded, he rose from his seat, and laying his hand impressively on my shoulder, said, "My son, if thou art of the Protestant religion, and art called upon, by the despotic rulers of this land, to abjure thy faith, remember the Lollards of Lud Church, and stand firm." I thanked him for his advice, and desired him to show me the grave of the unfortunate Alice. "Thou hast sat in the shadow of the tree which grows over it," he replied. I turned to the oak and broke off a leaf from its broad branches, which I deposited in my bosom, as a memento. Then, thanking the venerable old man again, I mounted my horse and rode away, my mind filled with sorrowful reflections.

*****

Ludchurch is situated in the centre of the *Back Forest*, which anciently formed part of the *Forest of Leek*. Belonging, after the Conquest, to the Earls of Chester, this district with Swythamley was granted by Randle de Blunderville to the Abbey Dieu-la-cresse, and it continued attached to that foundation until the dissolution, in 1538, when it passed to the Crown, 5th May, 32 Henry VIII, by whom a grant of it was made to Wm. Trafford, of Wymslow, Esquire.

.

THE WILDS OF CHESHIRE

Game birds; Saxon cemetery at Butley; history of Macclesfield Forest; tornado in Macclesfield Forest 1662; scenery, climate and natural history; small farmers of Macclesfield Forest; Wildboarclough; 'Peregrine' and falconry; fishing in the Dane: Shutlingslow, a former beacon site.

Stretching away in our front and over the river Dane, are what have been aptly termed by a friend of the writer, "the Wilds of Cheshire," who describes how there are bad roads, and sometimes no roads, across the "wilds." There are hills, streams, rocks and moorland, but few trees; and, in consequence of the altitude, very short summers.

England may have wilder parts, as in Yorkshire and in counties further north, where the scenery is rougher and on a larger scale, but there is nothing further south more rudely beautiful, and there are some spots here as extraordinary and as well worth seeing as any in the Island. People who know only the southern counties, are sometimes surprised to hear that between them and Scotland - in the heart of England itself - there are red grouse in abundance, with plenty of heather, hills and even mountains. The red grouse - *Lagopus Scoticus*, or *Britannicus*, as Yarrell so properly suggests - is found nowhere but in the British Isles, - in England, Wales, Ireland and extensively in Scotland. This bird does not appear farther south than the north of Staffordshire; the heather of the southern counties holding black game, but not the red grouse.

In describing the "Wilds of Cheshire," or what are so called, it is requisite to embrace a strip of Derbyshire and a small portion of the north of Staffordshire.

Macclesfield Forest, which lies in the very heart of the "wilds," and which is mentioned in Ormerod's "History of Cheshire," was at one time exceedingly extensive, but the district now called by that name is said not much to exceed ten thousand acres. The old forest seems to have been in existence before the Doomsday survey was made; and the Saxons - thane and serf - who sought refuge in it after the Conquest, gave the Normans some trouble.

An old cemetery was discovered at Butley, near Prestbury, not very long ago, which the learned in such matters declare to have been crammed with Saxon corpses, after a slaughter rather more wholesale than was even then common. The stones had been subjected to great heat, and a substance was found on them which was supposed to be blood. The history of the forest is probably something as follows: - before the Conquest, the whole neighbourhood of Macclesfield belonged to the famous Earl Edwin, against whom William had a peculiar enmity. The scattered Saxons fled for refuge to the wilds of the forest, formed themselves into disciplined bands, and, in their turn, plundered their oppressors. But the Norman Earls of Chester displaced them, and created an office of Master Forester, which carried with it the power of life and death; and Sir Vivian de Davenport, the first Master, adopted for his crest a *felon's head, haltered.* The lawless bands who inhabited the forest suffered by the vigilance of these Masters and their eight subordinates. Two shillings and a salmon were given for the capture of a "master-robber," and one shilling for any member of his troop. But the time came when this excessive power passed away, and the Masters were succeeded by stewards, who, (Ormerod tells us) "were appointed and removed at pleasure, until the reign of Edward IV." Then it was that the forest came into the hands of the Stanley family, with whom it remains now, has remained since, with this exception, that Oliver Cromwell gave it to Sir William Brereton, from whom it returned to the Stanleys at the Restoration.

There are very few trees in Macclesfield Forest, and scarcely any that have not been recently planted. In 1662, an event occurred which, if the account given of it in "Admirable Curiosities" is to be at all relied on, was very extraordinary. "July 20th, 1662, was a very stormy and tempestuous day in many parts of Cheshire and Lancashire .... The same day in the forest of Maxfield" - Macclesfield - "in Cheshire, there arose a great pillar of smoke, in height like a steeple, and judged twenty yards broad, which, making a most hideous noise, went along the ground six or seven miles, levelling all in the way. It threw down fences, also stone walls, and carried the stones a great distance from their places; but happening on moorish ground not inhabited, it did the less hurt. The terrible noise it made so frightened the cattle, that they ran away, and were thereby preserved. It passed over a corn-field, and laid it as even with the ground as if it had been trodden down by feet. It went through a wood and turned up above an hundred trees by the roots; coming into a field full of cocks of hay ready to be carried in, it swept all away, so that scarce a handful of it could afterwards be found; only it left a great tree in the middle of the field, which it had brought from some other place. From the forest of Maxfield it went up by a town called Taxal, and thence to Waily - "Whaley" - Bridge, where, and nowhere else, it overthrew an house or two; yet the people that were in them received not much hurt, but the timber was carried away nobody knew whither. From thence it went up the hills into Derbyshire, and so vanished."

The scenery of this neighbourhood reminds one of that of the Scotch Highlands, but in miniature. Hills - mountains - crags, heather, bilberries, rushes, peat, burns, a pure invigorating air, mists in season and sometimes out of season, scattered cottages, sheep, stone walls - these are some of the characteristics of the "Wilds of Cheshire". The winters are long and white, but not exceptionally cold. Sometimes we have great storms of wind, when no one could live on the hill-tops. We have little spring, but the summer is generally beautiful, and so is the autumn. In May there are a hundred great banks, blue with the wild hyacinth, or bright with the first green of the bracken fern. Later on, there are skies bluer than the banks, with a hot sun, which drives the cattle to the brooks; and the country, which in winter does not hold a bird besides grouse, a few partridges, a snipe and a passing crow, is full of the song and the presence of summer visitants. The hills stand about us, and shut out a distant view, but you can climb them and look over forty miles into Wales. By the 12th of August the heather is purple and smells like honey; the hot air comes off the crags, and you see it mixing with a cooler atmosphere all along the hill; the tributaries to the one large brook shine as they come down their irregular beds; the shepherd, for once in his life, calls his dog to heel, and keeps the wall as he passes on; the grouse lie for this day, and perhaps for the next, almost like partridges in the south; and we labour along till the evening, in our dreamed-of, hoped-for, prayed-for, magnificent toil.

There are not many partridges on these hills, and they are smaller and darker in plumage than the southern birds. Snipe breed here, but are not so numerous as they were some years ago. Pewits are here in quantities in the spring and summer, and the young afford good sport with a dog that is used to them. The golden plover is seen in the autumn, but not often. Curlews occasionally breed on the moors, and woodcocks have been seen during the summer in some of the big woods on the Swythamley property adjoining, which indicates the probability that they, also, occasionally breed there.

The inhabitants of the forest and its neighbourhood are small farmers who work, for the most part, with their own hands, some of them keeping two or three servants. With a few exceptions they are ignorant and penurious. They lounge along the country and up the hills with long, slow strides; and, if they chance to meet a neighbour, they can hardly make up their minds to part with him for twenty minutes or

Wildboarclough

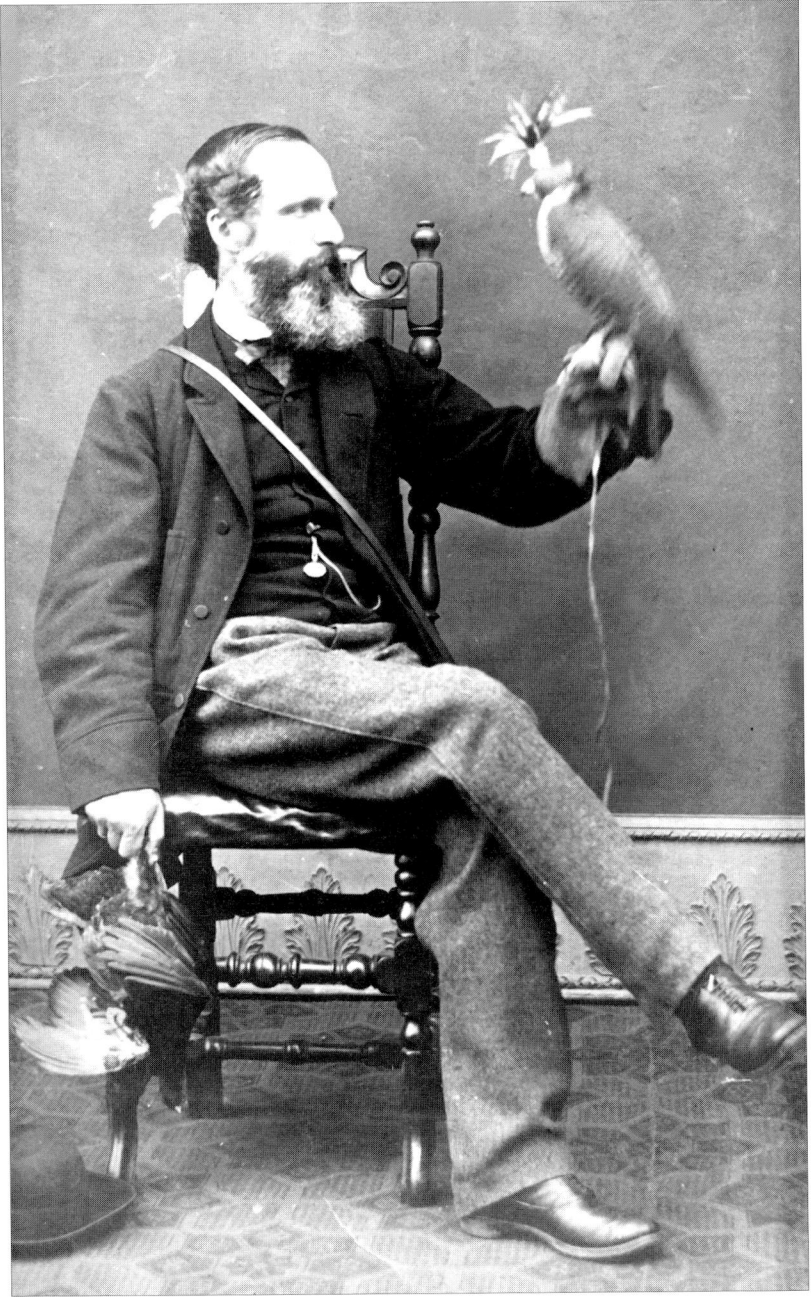

'Peregrine'

half an hour. They are a fine, sturdy set, but they want energy.

The tremendous ravine which reaches out some distance from the present forest is called Wild Boar Clough. Here are some scattered farmhouses, and here is the parsonage. The clergyman has two churches under his care, and receives for his labours the use of a house and rather less than £140 a year. There is a tale, believed by some of the people, of a wild-boar hunt which took place here not quite two hundred years ago. The boar was killed some distance from the Clough, at a place called "Kill Hill." There is an old farmhouse in the forest called "The Chamber," which is said to be built on the site of a hunting box used by the Kings of England-none, perhaps, of later date than Edward IV. "*Peregrine*," the *nom de plume* of a gentleman well known to excel in the noble art of falconry, which sport he has brought to perfection in these wilds, and from whose interesting description of his hunting grounds in the "far interior" I am quoting, tells us that - "the excellence of a peregrine, in game-hawking, is that it should fly as high as possible. Hence, perhaps, the origin of the term 'high-flyer,' as applied to others than hawks. For the falcon is put on the wing before the grouse or partridges rise, and she should get up eighty or a hundred yards before they are sprung. I have seen some of my hawks a quarter of a mile high, when you might have taken the bird for a boy's kite, 'waiting on' me and the dog most patiently. Then comes a dead point from the dog, and you hasten to spring the game; or you wake up an old cock grouse which goes off crowing, and with that curious twist in his flight which grouse-shooters know so well. Down comes the falcon from her pitch; you hear the rush of her wings as she passes high over you to the quarry. If the grouse be immediately under her when he rises, he will probably be dashed to the ground amidst a cloud of feathers, as her great foot rips up his back; or his wing may be broken; or - especially if he has been flown before - he may drop backwards on the heather untouched from under her very feet. Then she is at a disadvantage. But she sails round, and perhaps tries to hit him on the ground. Most likely he gets up, and is off at a terrible pace, while she, with her long wings, must get into her swing before she can hope to reach him. But if he is not hit, and does not fall without a blow when she stoops, a most exciting race begins, which is for life or death. His wings now work away with most rapid strokes; now he closes them for two seconds, and passes through the air like a bullet; now they strike even quicker than before. If you are standing on a stone wall as he goes by, he is away before you can exclaim. His round, dark form rushes past as the noise of his feathers rings in your ears. It is the very best pace of all; it is almost inconceivably rapid: it is for dear life. But she; - her stoop from the clouds brings her close behind him; it gives her a fearful impetus; she is simply flying him down, and knows that he is dying before her. Yet he may live - not in fair flight, not from excess of speed; but he may live still. There is a mountain burn near at hand; it is shallow now, but its banks have been undermined by the winter rains, and the heather droops over them like a screen. Under them at once, good grouse, for you deserve your life; you have struggled half a mile to save it. There is no dog near to put you out; no marker to tell tales about you. True, she may 'wait on' above you - 'make her point,' as they say; but you are a good way off the falconer, and something else will be put up before he reaches you. I think you are pretty safe. But if no such friendly cover is found - and there is uncommonly little time in which to select it - the grouse dies, either cut over by the falcon, or taken by her as he drops by a wall-side, with some indefinite sort of hope of getting between the stones."

The river Dane divides the Cheshire side of the "wilds" from Swythamley. There are some bits in this river most exquisitely picturesque: overhanging trees, huge boulders, towering moss-capped rocks, low and most likely-looking waterfalls for the speckled trout, are level with you or above you, as you wade, fly-rod in hand, up this splendid stream. A fly can be thrown in nearly every part, and a minnow can be spun anywhere. Big trout are occasionally taken, but the generality run small. We have also pools in the neighbourhood, well stocked with fish.

A pack of harriers, with a mounted huntsman and whip, the presence of every English game bird, excepting the capel-calzie, together with coursing and the royal pursuit of falconry, makes the sporting of this part of England almost unique. The late Earl of Derby, himself a warm admirer of field sports, gave the fish and game of this noble manor to the Squire of Swythamley, by whom it was strictly preserved for nearly a quarter of a century, until death removed his generous friend, and England lost one of her greatest statesmen.

Drayton sings:-

"*Bollin*, that along doth nimbler *Birkin* bring,
From *Maxfield's mightie wildes*, of whose shagged *sylvan's* shee
Hath in the rocks been woo'd their paramour to be;
Who in the darksome holes and caverns kept her long,
And that proud forest made a party to her wrong."

Shutlingslow, in the forest, is the highest hill in Cheshire, and was formerly a beacon station, fires being lit on its summit in times of war or expected invasion. The chief object of interest to those who ascend it, is the spring of water on the top, and the fine view it affords. The modern Forest of Macclesfield contains few vestiges of its ancient woods and "mightie wildes"; and from its appearance no traveller would suppose, as he crosses its mountain solitudes or shelters under its tottering stone walls from the sweeping blast, that the fawn and the deer had pastured there, or that the outlaw and his "merrie men" had ever found the smallest pittance by the plunder of its few inhabitants.

SWYTHAMLEY

Hanging Stone, an ancient hill altar; Swythamley deer park; Swythamley Hall destroyed by fire 1813; contents of present Hall; dining and ball room for tenantry; Burke the mastiff; pleasure grounds; stables; gamekeeper's sanctum; kennels; workshops.

The notable projecting rock called the *Hanging Stone* is situated about a mile to the W.N.W. of Ludchurch, on the brow of the pine-covered hill above Swythamley Park, and almost overhangs the road running from Flash, by Castle Cliffs, over the Back Forest. A short path, striking to the north out of this road, brings us by a steep ascent to the foot of the stone. Thomas Loxdale, the antiquarian vicar of Leek, visited it in 1708, and speaks of it as probably a greater wonder than either the Roches, "one of the most romantic prospects in nature," or Ludchurch, "of which Plot gives a very accurate description." "It consists," he continues, in his letter to the Bishop, (Shaw, II. 1.) "of two flat stones, laid table-wise upon the brow of a precipice, resting (as may plainly be seen), upon other large ones that lie near the centre, from which supporters they shoot out, perhaps seven or eight feet to the south, being elevated, at the extremity, above the surface of the declining hill, some thirty feet. The other part must be proportionally large to balance the immense weight of this overhanging end, and prevent its slipping down the bank. I imagine it to be much larger (tho' I had no opportunity to examine it, it being covered with earth), and that this has drawn it a little from off its first horizontal place. Its being in part covered is owing to the nature of the adjacent earth, which is a black, oozy, peat soil. This, instead of being washed and worn away by wind and rain, as better land that lies high is observed to do, swells, and grows higher, as may be seen in the peat-pits so common in this country. The neighbours look upon all these to remain in the same condition they were left in by the Flood; and as to most of them they are no doubt in the right; but, that these are so I cannot agree, because the bulk, shape and position are exactly the same; the levels and squares the same; all of which, in my opinion, bespeak a design, such regularity being rarely seen in works of chance."

Mr Loxdale next goes on to discuss the probable use of the Hanging Stone, supposing it to be an artificial structure; and at length arrives at the conclusion that it may possibly be "an old *Charemluach*, or one of the ancients' *devoted stones*, or *hill altars*, on which their sacrifices were offered." Gold, silver and copper coins were discovered in 1834, by Mr Hughes, a forester of Mr Brocklehurst, not far from the base of the Hanging Stone, while preparing holes for a new plantation; one was a Cannon Mint piece, value 30d., made from old cannons; others of the time of the civil wars between York and Lancaster, and a gold coin of a much earlier date, probably one of the Edwards'. Descending the hill-side, and traversing a few green pastures, we find ourselves at the head gamekeeper's lodge, a cottage embowered in ivy, with its little garden of quaint square-cut yew hedges, where a noble, tawny mastiff, the poachers' foe, lies basking idly in the sun. Large flocks of wild ducks are flying to and fro, from pond and stream; and the spotted fallow deer are quietly grazing in the well-timbered undulating Park; for Swythamley is one of the *seventeen* deer parks of Staffordshire, as described by Mr Evelyn Philip Shirley, M.A., F.S.A., in his interesting work, called the "Deer and Deer Parks of England."

The origin of the Park lies in obscurity, but in the work alluded to, it is mentioned how "Swythamley was an ancient Grange to the Abbey of Dieulacres, and 'Parke-land,' near Swythamley Grange, occurs in a lease granted in the twenty-ninth of Henry VIII, and that deer have always been kept there." They are of the spotted menil breed, and the venison is remarkable for its fine quality.

The greater portion of the Hall was burnt down on December 26th, 1813, at the commencement of the Long Frost. It was then an old gabled mansion, built upon the site of the original Grange; but the present structure, though large and convenient, has no artistic beauty to recommend it, and its grey stone walls are mainly overgrown with ivy. The views from some of the windows are wild and picturesque, embracing a wide range of heather-covered hills, dotted with dark pine woods. The entrance hall contains some of the carving rescued from the fire in 1813, one side being covered with a fine example of Goblein tapestry formerly in the possession of the late Duke of Sussex. Trophies of fallow deer killed in the Park hang round. One splendid specimen, counting forty points and remarkable for its breadth of palmated horn, is undoubtedly finer than any that have been shot of late years. Above the ancient oaken mantle shelf is a magnificent head of a red stag. It is a royal, of eleven tines, and was shot by Mr Philip Brocklehurst, on October 7th, 1869, after a severe stalk of several hours through a difficult and thickly wooded country: it was late in the evening before a shot could be obtained; the "muckle harte" stood with nose upraised, winding his pursuers, when the fatal bullet entered his throat, causing him to rear and fall headlong down a rocky precipice into the river Dane, on the Cheshire side of Whitelee Farm. The stag was of enormous size, weighing upwards of twenty stone, and had been roaming for some time among the forests and moorlands round Swythamley.

The house contains many objects worthy of notice either to the antiquarian or the artist: weapons of various nations, curiosities brought back from travel, ivory tankards of the sixteenth and seventeenth centuries, with rare and valuable antiques (several of great local interest), rent-rolls unintelligible except to savants versed in early

English, and manuscripts beautifully engrossed long prior to the invention of printing.

The paintings are chiefly studies from the denizens of field or forest, portraying much talent, with a thorough knowledge of their haunts and habits; portraits of favourite dogs and horses, who have earned a reputation that has made them worthy of the place they occupy; while here and there is a choice drawing by some well-known master. In the centre of the servants' offices is a large and lofty room, measuring thirty feet by sixty, used as a dining and ball-room for the tenantry, who twice a year, to the number of a couple of hundred, assemble on the occasion of the rent audits to dine and devote the evening to the enjoyment of dancing, amateur concerts and music. In describing a little of the interior, we must not omit to mention the *house guardian*, who accompanied us in our inspection. This companion was no other than a magnificent noble black and tan mastiff, with markings as perfect as a ladies' toy-terrier, but whose massive head, intelligent stern eye, broad, expansive chest, and strong muscular limbs produced an impression that we would rather meet as friends than foes. There are few things more irritating to one who consistently honours dogs as I do, than to hear superficial and indiscriminate people talk of those animals as if they were all alike in their mental and moral qualities, or perhaps confide to you that "they like dogs in their proper place" (to wit, somewhere out of sight). He who has once loved a dog, if he find courage after its loss to seek a second friend, nearly always endeavours to procure one of the same breed, and, if possible, the same family, for his heart is drawn to such an animal by its likeness to the dead. The quadruped I am describing is somewhat narrow-minded - a dog of one idea - and that idea is his master. To the rest of mankind he is somewhat reserved and indifferent. If reprimanded, he will shrink, hang his head, and convey by sad and solemn looks his sense that a cruel breach has been made in the harmony of the relations between himself and his

Hanging Stone

The Deer Park, Swythamley

Swythamley Hall - interior view

17th century Ivory Tankard from Swythamley Hall

Burke

In the Gamekeeper's Sanctum

Jim Sutton, Woodman

Hunting Trophy, Swythamley Hall

owner. After a time this wears off, and he will hasten to assure his friend that he is graciously forgiven for his bad temper, and that with all his faults, he loves him still. At mealtimes he will blink urbanely; but as it proceeds, and the dreadful idea occurs to him that the courses are over, the dinner ended and he unnoticed. He bears no malice, but subsides rapidly and resignedly into quiescence, and seeks ere long that peculiar consolation for unsatisfied longings which is to be found by rolling himself into the nearest approach to a circle attainable to the vertebrata. *Burke* (for that is the dog's Christian name, from an imaginary resemblance to a certain *life-taker*, who was the colleague of *Hare*, and engaged in the same business), except on days set apart for shooting, seems to live in an atmosphere of "refined and gentle melancholy." His great, mournful eyes look as if they might at any time overflow with drops from the depths of a divine despair, and only when he lays his noble head sadly on the tablecloth, and unmistakably turns those eloquent orbs in unutterable longing towards his favourite dish, are we able to fathom the profundity of his sorrow and his aspirations. He has an oriental indifference for all proceedings not immediately concerning himself, and habitually lies down to enjoy his "kef" on the rug, seeming to regard with pitying indulgence the fuss which two-legged creatures make about trifles disconnected with the real concerns of life - namely *sport* and *dinner*. This dog, who really loves his master, delights in mere propinquity, likes to lie down on the floor, resting against his feet, better than on a cushion a yard away, and after a caress or two asks no more, but sleeps quietly in perfect contentment. A short, tender touch from his tongue to hands or face, corresponding to his feelings as kisses of affection do to ours, is all the recognition he permits himself to give on the return of his master from a journey; but on discovering his absence, "Burke" will wander with a despairing look from room to room in quest of his lost friend, and failing to find him, will pull to the floor a game-bag or some article he has seen him use or wear, upon which he will stretch himself and patiently wait his coming. He is an excellent retriever of game or water-fowl, either by land or water, and passionately fond of the gun, and has been known to work so industriously during the beating of a large woodcock covert in the Back Forest as to require carting home in the evening, being quite unable to walk unassisted. In the billiard room is a clever painting in oil, life-size, of this faithful animal, who bears a deservedly high reputation in the neighbourhood for courage and intelligence. From a terrace walk on the south side of the Hall can be seen a piece of water in the dell below, frequented by hundreds of wild ducks, and an extensive rookery follows the sides of a long rugged ravine, through which a trout stream winds, often the haunt of the solitary and wandering heron. Wild fowl breed here in security, but on the larger sheets of water a mile or two away, where there is denser harbour of bulrush and sedges, their lives are no longer respected by the sportsman.

> "Down close! the wild ducks come, and darting down,
> Throw up on every side the troubled wave,
> Then gaily swim around with idle play.
> With breath restrained and levelled gun,
> He views their movements.
>
> With fiery burst,
> The unexpected death invades the flock;
> Trembling they lie, and beat the plashing pool,
> While those remoter from the fatal range
> Of the wild shot, mount up on vigorous wing,
> And wake the sleeping echoes as they fly."

The pleasure grounds are more assisted by Dame Nature than art; waterfalls, splashing fountains, shady dells, purling brooks and grassy walks bordered with the bluebell and foxglove; here and there long vistas of scarlet-coloured rhododendrons growing amidst sturdy oaks, over whose heads some centuries have passed; hares and pheasants, some of the latter of snow-white plumage, and now and then a stray fawn, dash suddenly into sight, and as quickly vanish amidst the tall and waving fern. A curious brass sun-dial, date 1645, was found in the old gardens a few years since, which may possibly have been consulted by hungry Cromwellite soldiers in anticipation of the Swythamley dining hour, on their march at that period through the district, the same day, perhaps, that the persecuted old squire took refuge in the barn, laying about him with his flail, shouting "now thus," and mentally wishing the backs of his unwelcome visitors were feeling its weight.

The stables are much the same as in the days the country was hunted by old Squire Trafford and his gallant pack. They consist of a large quadrangular stone building and belfry, overgrown with ivy, with accommodation for about eighteen horses. In the centre is a courtyard, entered by a covered archway, requiring a little extra neat steering before the well-appointed team of four short-legged browns can be piloted to their stable doors. Everything is beautifully kept, and the chief saddle-room, adorned with bright bits, steel pole chains, well polished brass harness, and a few appropriate sporting sketches, is a credit to the artistic taste of the head groom.

The gamekeeper's sanctum is somewhat a curiosity: here we find weapons of deadly construction, captured from poachers in some midnight conflict. Six-feet quarter staves, inlaid with sharp knife blades, for the severing of the fingers or muscles from the hand that might grasp it in the struggle for mastery; man-traps, with teeth inches long, that fifty years ago were permitted to seize and lacerate the victim's leg, while other engines of a similar description, but so designed that, though effectually locking themselves round the ankle of the marauder, hold him without penetrating the flesh. Nets of intricate nature adorn the walls, some for the pool and river, and others for fur and feather. Helmets and shields of wickerwork, truncheons, staves and implements for offence and defence strew the floor; all around us is a medley of things appertaining to the sports of the field; but not wishing to show our ignorance of the craft by further inquiry, we thank our stalwart conductor, cased in cords and fustian, and retire. Passing the dog-kennels, which are compactly arranged into four separate apartments with exercising yards, each being well filled with setters and pointers, spaniels, terriers and lion-coloured mastiffs, we come to the workshops for the estate: here there is a forge, with its bright, glowing furnace; next to it are boiling and steaming houses, where food for the kennels and cart stables is prepared; then a joiner's shop, and further on again, a lathe-room, with cases filled with intricate and complicated implements for manipulating in brass, ivory or wood. The machinery is all turned by a turbine, and everything is done on the premises, from making a wheelbarrow to building a farmhouse. The steward's office adjoins the lathe and saw department, so that all proceeds under his management and supervision.

THE ROACHES

Turner's Pool, a monastic fishpond; Hanging Stone, a Druidical cromlech; rocking stone; Doxy Pool; Hen Cloud; Royal visit to the Roaches, 1872; Rock Hall, a cave dwelling; Bess Bowyer, reputed descendent of mosstroopers; Windygates.

Turner's Pool (Thornehurst's pole), one of the resorts of the wild fowl, is mentioned in the royal grant by King Henry VIII, to Wm. Trafford, A.D. 1534, and, according to Loxdale, was no doubt constructed by the monks of Dieulacre, for the purpose of a stew, or fishpond; the fine trout, exceeding 5lb. in weight, captured in it even at the present day being of a size and flavour that denote they have not much degenerated from the time when, a few hundred years ago, their ancestors were served up at the board of my lord abbot and his lusty friars. Here, in full view, are those high stony grounds called the "Roaches," that made King James say, Staffordshire was "only fit to be cut out into thongs, to make highways for the rest of the kingdom."

Their bold and varied outline, backed by heathery moors, adds much to the general picturesqueness of the country. Plot, in the "Compleat History of Staffordshire," published 1730, jots down - "When I came to Leek and saw the Hen-cloud and Leek roches (some of them kissing the clouds with their tops and running along in mountainous ridges for some miles together), my admiration was still heightened to see such vast rocks and such really stupendous prospects, which I had never seen before, or could have believed to have been anywhere, but in picture."

In 1860 was constructed a path or track along the whole length of the Roaches, on nearly the highest ridge, which can be easily travelled by a mule or pony, and which often yields a pleasant excursion to explorers. Objects of interest are to be found near this road, amongst which is an old heathen altar or *Druidical Cromlech*, which viewed from its interior is very curious; not far from this is a large rock, many tons in weight, but so wonderfully balanced that a lady might easily rock it with her foot; a few yards from the *rocking stone* is a circular cutting, level with the ground, about which many conjectures have been raised: it is in the solid rock, but why or wherefore it was made is still a mystery. Following the pony track we shortly come upon the margin of a small *tarn*, called *Doxy Pool*, dark and deep, many hundred feet above any known spring in the district, and which, no matter how hot the summer, is always full to the brink. This is a favourite drinking place for the grouse, and the soft sand near the water's edge, is often found covered with the impress of their numerous footmarks. A mile or so farther on the *Hen Cloud* rears its noble head, showing many tints and shades of green and grey on the broken slopes near the peak, while to the right, deep down, stretches a pine wood flourishing in its early growth. Here is one of the wildest and most beautiful spots in North Staffordshire, and having been recently visited by royalty, a description of the occurrence may assist in picturing the scene.

A local journal, in describing the royal visit to Swythamley, on August 23rd, 1872, says:- "For the first time since the visit of Mary, Queen of Scots, royalty passed through the ancient town of Leek. In every town in England, or any other country where true loyalty and patriotism prevails, the visit of the sovereign, or any of the royal personages allied to the sovereign, is always considered to be an occasion of importance and is generally remembered with pleasure by those who witness it. Her Royal Highness the Princess Mary of Cambridge and the Prince Teck have for the past few days honoured the Earl and Countess of Shrewsbury with their company at Alton, and on

Wednesday last notification was sent to the authorities in Leek, that their Royal Highnesses, along with a distinguished party, would pass through Leek, weather permitting, about noon on Friday." The occasion of their coming was to grace with their presence a picnic given by Mr Brocklehurst, of Swythamley, at his moorland shooting lodge.

Rock Hall, the place selected, is situated in the midst of the wild romantic crags and rocky precipices of the far-famed Roaches, whose jagged forms and majestic situations have been the subject of the author's study, the poet's song, and the sage's lore. Everything was done by way of alteration and repairs - for the rugged and huntsman-like road required it for the reception of such visitors - that could possibly be devised to make the task of ascending the naturally difficult summit as easy and comfortable as possible. Nor did the preparations for the reception of their Royal Highnesses stop here; flags floated in the breeze from different prominent positions, the royal standard waved conspicuously on the verge of the third summit, and the display of bunting generally was profuse, and had a fine effect. At this point tents had been erected, one of which, having two huge pieces of rock forming the gable ends, the interior decorated with pink and white heather and carpeted with the skins of wild animals, was especially dedicated to royalty.

The Roaches command a view of the country for miles round, and their cragged peaks and romantic surroundings are often the subject of geological comment. The Roach ascended by the royal party has, as it were, four divisions or summits, which can be reached by means of a circuitous route up a flight of steep steps cut out of the solid rock. Facing the edge of the rock on the third summit, and immediately close to the royal standard, was the seat of honour for her Royal Highness. This was constructed by a huge hollow being hewn into the rock; in the hollow cushions were placed, the surroundings being covered with white satin, embroidered with the royal arms, and guarded round the face of the rock with a slender chain.

Shortly after 12 o'clock anxious visitors began to crowd about Leek station, and housewives who had dispensed with domestic duties *pro tempore* enjoyed with their children a leisure hour, and betook themselves to their gardens, house windows, or anywhere else where a view of the approaching procession could be obtained. With the royal visitors came royal weather, the sun shone with unusual brilliance and strength, the sky was clear and unclouded; consequently, the concourse of people was larger than otherwise it might have been, and they preserved their good temper and loyalty under a scorching sun perhaps better than they would have done under a wetting rain. Shortly after one o'clock the iron horse - a special train from Alton, consisting of a saloon carriage and three first-class carriages - steamed up into the station, a *feu de joie* being fired as they approached, the rifle band playing from the bridge "God save the Queen."

The procession, which was composed of nine carriages, started about half-past one from the station, and making a computation of the crowd that swarmed the bridge and lined the streets, there would not be fewer than from 8,000 to 9,000 turned out to witness the cavalcade, who, upon the approach of the royal party, at intervals cheered lustily; and what with the outriders in their well-known scarlet tunics, the equerries in waiting, Captain Dausey and Mr Clement, the bays and greys, the superb and extensive decorations, which had a gorgeous effect in the glittering sunbeams, the scene had a grand effect and one that will not be forgotten by the inhabitants of Leek, and those from Macclesfield and elsewhere who witnessed it, for many years to come. The procession was headed by Lord Shrewsbury's brass band, under the superintendence of Mr Forester, and followed by the Leek Rifles, under the command of Lieutenant Sleigh and Ensign Worthington, and also by the fine band of the corps. The route chosen was up Canal Street and Great Edward Street, through the sheep market and into the Market Place, and here the crowd was so dense that it was with great difficulty the procession could cut through the living mass.

Arrived at Rock Hall, after a beautiful drive through a romantic country of five miles, the royal party were received by Philip Brocklehurst, Esq., and Miss Brocklehurst. A pony carriage was in waiting, in which her Royal Highness and Lady Shrewsbury took seats, and were conveyed as far as the steep, sloping, rugged mounds betokened it was safe to go. The royal party then proceeded on foot, and after a circuitous route - a route which it was evident within the past few days had undergone considerable alterations to render it safely passable - among the living rocks of the far-famed Roaches their Royal Highnesses and the distinguished party arrived at what we may call their destination, the third summit of the Roach. The Princess displayed capital mountaineering powers, and during a portion of the ascent the Duke of Teck gallantly adjusted a rope for her support.

After luncheon the Earl of Shrewsbury said he was desired by her Royal Highness to offer only one toast on that occasion, and that was to propose the health of Mr Philip Brocklehurst and Miss Brocklehurst. It would be difficult for him to express their gratitude for the manner they had been received, and the way in which everything had been done. Her Royal Highness desired him to again return her very cordial thanks. Their Royal Highnesses accompanied with a few - a very few - distinguished visitors then ascended the highest summit of the Roach and enjoyed the excellent view of the surrounding country it affords. Royal salutes were fired during the stay, and having spent fully three hours on the Roaches, the royal party descended to the cave, where they inscribed their names, and near to the entrance of which the Princess graciously planted a Scotch fir tree to commemorate her visit. To show their loyalty and respect, the labourers on the estate made a "path" for a few yards approaching the royal carriage by strewing their coats on the green sward, so that their Royal Highnesses might step from these into the carriage. On the Princess being informed that this was the

The Roaches

Hen Cloud

Princess Mary of Cambridge

Prince of Teck

Royal Picnic on the Roaches, 1872

Rock Hall

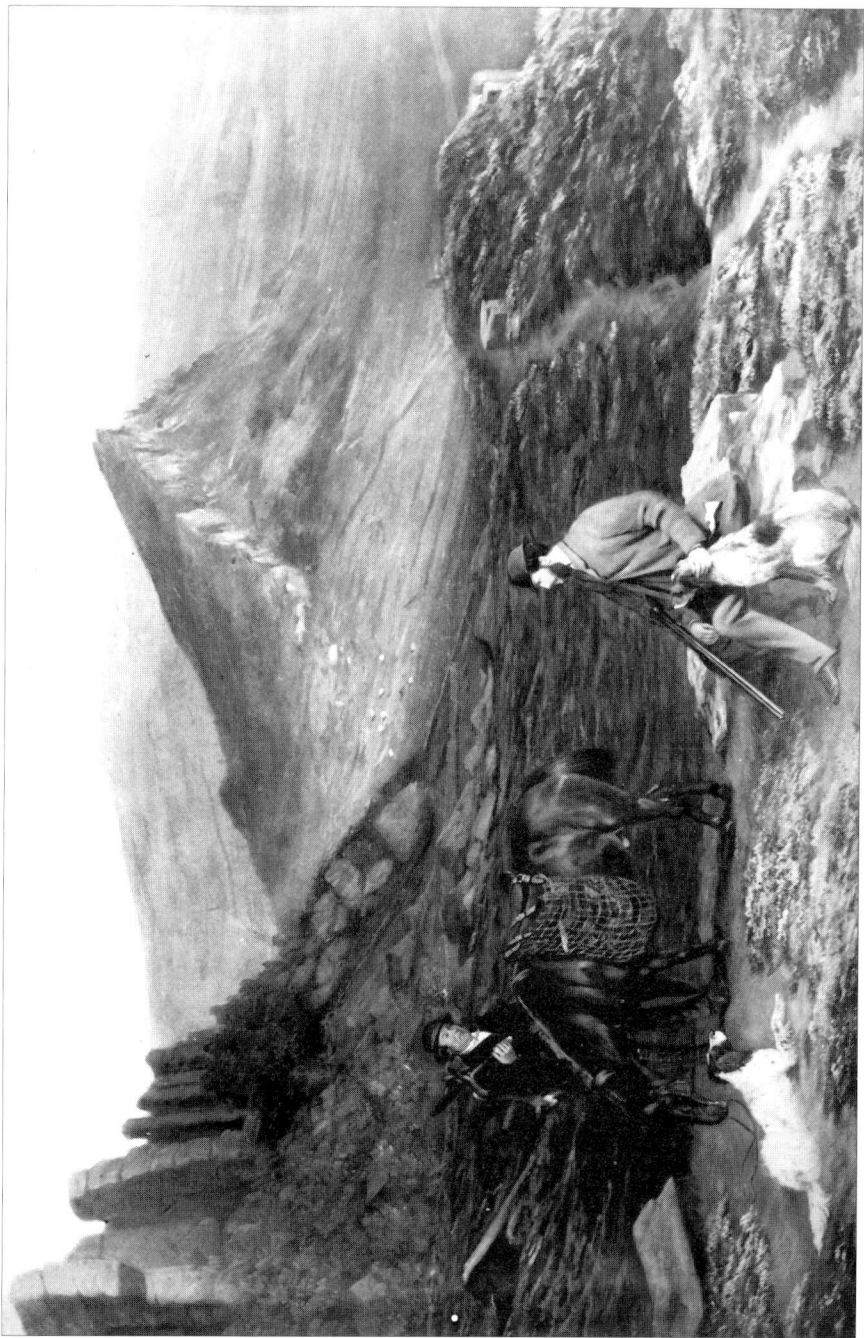

Sir Philip Brocklehurst and Jim Barber (Gamekeeper) on the Roaches, 1867

voluntary work principally of the labourers on the estate, her Royal Highness expressed how much this exhibition of loyalty and good feeling had touched her, and in bidding adieu expressed the pleasure she had derived from her visit amongst the wild scenery of the Roaches.

> "A kennelled hound betrays th' abode of man;
> Rock-hall its name; part cave, part stone-built lodge;
> Where dwells the lusty keeper who protects
> The furred and feathered tenants of these wilds
> From midnight raid of lawless poachers; who
> With net, and bag, and silent lurcher, would,
> Unchecked, their numbers thin. Nor does he fail,
> Should fortune bring the hawk within the range
> Of his unerring aim, to call him quick to book,
> For misdeeds dire against HIS code of laws.
>   Outside the cave
> A buxom matron in the free air plied
> Domestic duties. Near, her rosy babes
> Disported on the turf. In front, what seemed
> An ancient British barrow, petrified,
> A view of Merebrook furnished from its top,
> Approached by well cut steps."

The *cave dwelling*, called Rock Hall, was, until some score of years ago, occupied by an old crone of great age, known as Bess Bowyer. Here, in the large natural cavern, she lived for nearly a century, an immense mass of rocks having so fallen as to form the roof, sides and entrance. This she divided into two apartments, one for day and the other for night, and through both of which flowed a small ice-cold stream of water. In her weird-looking bedroom was a secret outlet, conducting among the wild crags at the back of the dwelling, and through which she assisted smugglers and deserters to escape from soldiers sent to capture them. During a portion of her life in the cave, a young and handsome girl, her *reputed* daughter, lived with her, but about whose history much mystery and doubt existed. The girl had a fine voice, and could be heard on summer nights among the rocks singing sadly to herself songs that sounded foreign to English ears. One winter morning the old hag was seen in great distress. Strange men had seized and carried off her child. She never returned, and at last the supposed mother was herself discovered dead in her lonely home. This Bess Bowyer was a reputed descendant of "Bowyer of the Rocks," a noted moss-trooper. The old romances shed a halo of poetic lustre around these desperate wanderers over moss and moor. They were kings of the forest, and levied black mail on all comers, and it was to assist in suppressing their raids that Hugh Kevelioc, Earl of Chester, who from books and old authorities is supposed or known to have died in one of his hunting excursions to Swythamley, appointed Lupus de Davenport, of Bramall, as master forester of Leek and Macclesfield, with the powers of life and death, about which time their allusive crest was adopted: "A felon's head couped proper, haltered *or*". There were eight subordinate foresters, two of which were "Hugo Browster and Thomas Browne," for "Sutton ça Wincle." They had the liberty of fishing within the forests, and of taking foxes, hares, squirrels, *bawsons* (badgers), *musketts* and eagles (Lyson's *Mag. Brit.*, Cheshire). The manor of Sutton being in the purlieus of the forest, was formerly held by the service of free forestry, by which its owner was bound to follow the king's standard in war, with the same arms (bows and arrows) that he guarded the forest, and whilst he so attended, he was exonerated from the custody of his bailiwick. Many of the forest manors were held by this tenure. On the death of John le Scot, the last Earl, the forest of Macclesfield passed to the Crown. A little lower down than Rock Hall is the old farmhouse called *Windygates*, the ancient seat of the Burgs, or Broughs, and has "T. B., 1634," inscribed on its front. "A tenement and land in Frith demised to Robert Burgh and others" is specially excepted in Edward VI's grant to Sir Robert Bagnall. Frith is a Saxon term, signifying a woody vale between two hills, and such was Leek Frith till the monks destroyed the timber. Frith (Sax. *peace*) among the Saxons signified a wood, and many woods were held sacred, and were sanctuaries (Baily): but probably the monks cut down the trees to improve the land.

Meerbrook Church

Meerbrook had a chapel by 1537. In the middle of the nineteenth century it consisted of the west tower, chancel and nave shown here. T§he dormer window lit a gallery; the steps against the tower led to a former schoolroom. On the right of this photograph can be seen a central tower, behind which were a chancel and vestry, erected in 1870. This represents the first stage of the rebuilding of the church to a design by R Norman Shaw. By 1873 the west tower had been demolished and the nave rebuilt, with an entrance porch.

MEERBROOK AND GUN HILL

Rebuilding and reopening of Meerbrook chapel; phosphorescence on Gun Hill; John Naden hung in chains from gibbet; haunted stile; the balloon that fell on Gun Hill, 1826: old pack horse road; Thorneyleigh and the Armett family; Hazlewood House.

Near the Roaches is Merebrooke, a smiling country village. "Merbrucke" and "Merbrucke Chappell" is mentioned in deeds *temp.* Henry VIII, and Robert le Merebrock in 32nd, Henry III.

In the *Staffordshire Advertiser* of November 1st, 1873, was the following account of the opening of the beautiful, picturesque building, which now replaces the old chapel:-

"St Matthew's Church, Meerbrook, near Leek, the nave of which has recently been rebuilt, was opened yesterday, the body of the edifice being in every way worthy of the chancel which was erected about five years ago at the sole expense of Miss Condliffe, as a memorial of deceased members of that lady's family. The original church was erected, according to the testimony of a local historian, by Ralph Bagnall, Knight, in the reign of Queen Elizabeth, 'as well for and in consideration of Divine service of our Lord God to be ministered and celebrated therein, as for the easement of my soul's comfort, and also for the love and good will which I owe and beare to my beloved tenants and neighbours in the hamlett of Frithe, as in consideration that I and my heires for ever hereafter may be solemnly prayed for in Lord's dayes and feasts dayes by the priest there ministring or preaching the Word of God.' The same Knight and other worthy men subsequently contributed towards the endowment of the church, which in 1677 was licensed for baptisms, and in 1679 for burials.

"Meerbrook is situated on one of the ridges of millstone in the extensive valley between the Roches and Gun, and although the founding of the church dates back to such a remote period, it was not till 1859 that, under the Marquis of Blandford's Act, the Ecclesiastical Commissioners constituted Meerbrook a district parish, or chapelry. A somewhat singular manuscript says, 'The inhabitants have chosen the minister in times past, but seem to have lost that immunity.' We were not able to learn yesterday how the inhabitants lost their privilege of choosing their minister, but it appears that the present patron is the vicar of Leek, and the choice which he made in selecting the Rev W. Nicholson, the present rector, is evidently satisfactory to the villagers, by whom he is much esteemed as a faithful and zealous pastor.

"Without detailing the circumstances which have led to the rebuilding of the church (which will accommodate about 250) we may state that the new nave is in the same style and in harmony with the chancel and tower. The style of the church altogether is of the early 14th century period, with carefully-designed tracery windows. The walls are thick, and have been well built with local materials. The roof of the new nave is very strongly framed, showing all the timbers, and covered with Staffordshire red tiles. Much remains to be done, but the work has been so far advanced that the church, as already stated, was opened yesterday afternoon. Mr Paul Bailey, Wetley Rocks, has well and substantially executed the masonry, Messrs. Nixon doing the carpentering, and Mr Phillips the glazing. Mr Edward Ash, of Meerbrook, has supplied a pulpit and a font of artistic design, and both are executed with admirable skill, as might have been expected from one to whom the work was, in a great measure, a labour of love. Mr R. Norman Shaw, A.R.A., London, designed the neat and substantial edifice, for the re-erection of which the inhabitants owe no small amount of thanks to the Rev W. Nicholson, rector. The cost of the nave has been about £1,100.

"The first of the services was held at three o'clock in the afternoon, and there was a large congregation. The clergy who took part in conducting the service were the Rev W. Nicholson, the Rev B. Pidcock, vicar of St Luke's, Leek; the Rev C. H. Joberns, curate of St Luke's, Leek; and the Rev J. Barnes; the preacher being the Lord Bishop of Lichfield. Among the other clergy present were the Revds. M. Piddocke, vicar of Wincle; F. W. Piercy, Leek; E. Nixon, Delamere; J. E. Deacon, vicar of Leek; and W. Foster, vicar of Horton. The Bishop preached an earnest and practical sermon from Ephesians iii. 2. His Lordship referred to the opening of that church, in a state more fit for the purposes for which it was set apart than the edifice which previously stood there, as an occasion for rejoicing; and spoke of the duty of uniting together as one congregation of faithful people pledged to do good to their fellow men. At the close of the service a tea meeting was held in the schoolroom, and was well attended."

Passing through the village of Meerbrook and past the parsonage, we climb the long hill leading towards the top of *Gun* .

Plot, in his "History of Staffordshire," writes, "If one ride on Gun in a dark night, in so wet a season that a horse breaks thro' the turf and throws up this black, moist, spongy sort of earth, he seems to throw up so much fire, which lies shining upon the ground like so many embers; by the light whereof one horse may trace another, tho' at some distance, and it be never so dark; it continuing light upon the ground, and gradually dying away, for near a quarter of an hour." A large portion of Gun-side is still covered with heather, and tenanted by grouse, black game and snipe, while here and there a dark fir plantation breaks its dreary waste; on the crest of *Gun ridge*, two miles from Swythamley, commanding a panoramic view rarely matched for beauty, variety, and extent, there stands an ancient gibbet post, it is oak - strong, slightly twisted, much weather beaten, decayed and furrowed. Here it has remained since 1732, a guide and a warning to those travellers doomed to wander

<blockquote>"O'er moorlands and mountains, rude, barren and bare."</blockquote>

From this gibbet, during many years, hung *John Naden* in chains, for the horrid, barbarous and cruel murder of his master, Robert Brough, of White Lea Hall, in Swythamley in the parish of Prestbury, as he was returning from Leek fair, in June 1731; and there are people still living who can remember the irons heavily swinging from the cross-arm of the gallows-tree in the winter's blast. The tragedy took place on the by-road between Hawksley and Hollin Hall, in Heaton, at a gate crossing a brook with high banks and holly on either side. Naden, it appears, lay in ambush at this gate, and when Brough stooped to open it from his horse, the faithless servant felled him to the earth and dispatched him. Part of the gibbet was cut up into staves for a stile, and to this day the rustics dread crossing this stile after nightfall.

The following is copied from a Leek journal, and is an account of an event that evidently created great astonishment to the Gunites of the period:-

"THE BALLOON THAT FELL ON GUN IN 1826. - The balloon which started from Beverley in Yorkshire on Thursday, the 25th of May, 1826, fell upon Gun, near Leek, not far from where Naden was executed and gibbetted, gave great alarm to the inhabitants, as it was the first seen in that locality. There were about twenty men working in the by-roads at the time, who were much frightened. Some ran one way, and some ran another; one fell on his knees and said, 'Eh, Mester Divel, dunna ta' me; oim a goodly mon and a godly mon, and oim a saum singer i' Winkow Chapel.' One, more valiant than the rest, when the grappling irons had struck, went knife in hand and said he would 'let his inside out,' some of the others following in the rear; and acting accordingly, soon laid the monster at his feet. Then there was a scramble for the spoil, which consisted of a bottle of wine, a few biscuits and a small compass, which was quickly demolished by the heroic men. The balloon was then carried to Swythamley Hall, and lay there for a week, and was inspected by scores of people, until the owner, who had fallen out and dislocated his arm and otherwise shaken himself, came to fetch it away. To show something of the size of the balloon, we may say the diameter of the middle segment was 37 feet, and the perpendicular height 55 feet 6 inches."

Again quoting from Mr Berresford's interesting history of this portion of the country: he writes, that over *Gun* there can yet be traced one of the oldest *pack-horse* roads, passing to within sixty to seventy yards of Naden's gibbet, leading to Thornilee Old-Hag and *Turnhurst Pool*. A little to the south of this Pool lies a field whose brooklets run either way towards the Trent and Mersey; and near it, on the slope of Gun (anciently *Dunne*), lies *Thorneyleigh*, on the Swythamley estate, and once the residence of the venerable family of "Armett, Gentlemen." The name of Armett occurs in subsidy list of 37 Henry VIII and 14 April, 1 Edward VI. "Mrs Armett, of Thorneyleigh, 6th June, 1665, leaves charities to Leek and Meerbrook." Their old stone house still remains, with its mullioned windows, no mean index of what, they doubtless were - substantial franklyns at the least. There are these inscriptions, carved in stone: -

A

W A   G C

I C 1691   I C 1670

the first over a doorway opening into a garden, and the other over a door of an outhouse.

A still more pleasant memento may be found in a field to the south, viz., their old "pleasure grounds." A large and most beautiful grove of ancient hollies, which stands on the hill-side, and forms an irregular line, enclosing an oval space of some 200 yards long by 100 across, with clumps feathering to the ground, studding the interior. One may almost trace the old walks running amongst the luxuriant bushes, and a more charming task than to do so could scarcely be desired. Ash

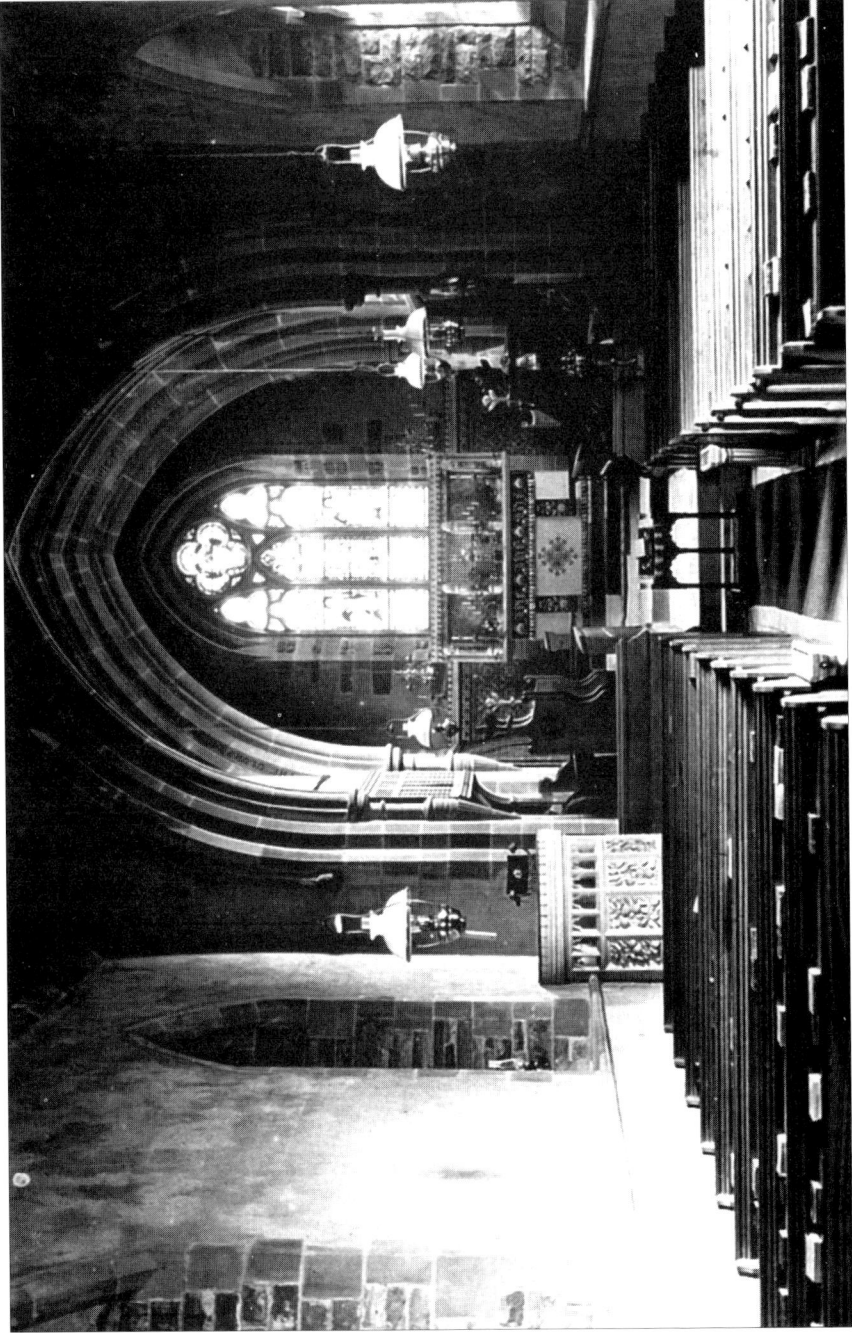

Interior, Meerbrook Church

trees, with their graceful forms, and "wickies," with bright, red berries, on whose stems the ivy mingles with wild roses, and seems to fall in graceful tangles to the earth. And as the evening approaches, myriads of birds, returning to their nightly shelter, vocalise the solitude, and drive away the gloomy thoughts which traces of long-departed and faded greatness are wont to inspire.

Another of their houses was *Toft Hall*, in Heaton, the residence of Wm. Armett, Esquire, who, about 1765, served the office of high sheriff for the county of Stafford.

The hill on which Thornyleigh stands, continues to rise till it attains the height. of 1,000 feet, and commands a fine view.

To the east, on the other side of the valley, in a brown, broken line, the Roaches rise 1670 feet above the sea, and from their either ends Axe-edge 1750 feet, Shutlingslow, 1686; Bosley Minns on the north, and Morridge, 1500 feet, on the south, break away into blue distance. The valleys lying between Gun and these hills, beautifully diversify the scene.

On the one side Swythamley, with its deer-dotted park; in front, Leek frith and its tiny sheets of water; and to the south, Leek, the moorland metropolis. Turning towards the west, one sees a broad, open vale, containing Horton, Rudyard, Endon and Rushton, bounded on the opposite side by a long hill, over which the castle-topped summit of Mow Cop 1090 feet, and blue ranges of distant Welsh and Cheshire hills, may be discerned. On the further side of Turnhurst or Turner's pool, is *Hazlewood House,* which, with its estate, has been lately added to Swythamley. The deeds, *temp.* Elizabeth, are in perfect preservation, as also a lease 29th Henry VIII, 16th July, in which Hazlewood House and Turnhurst pool are named, giving to Edward Lodge, of Haghmond, Salop, gentleman, "tymbre for fyrebote, howsebote, heybote and cartebote," and be allowed to "rydd, forke and grubb" all trees and underwood.

Gig Hall

WINCLE, AND RELICS OF ANCIENT TIMES

Whitelee and Gig Hall; the history of Wincle Grange, a paper read in 1853; Barleighford: the Bridestones; Clulow Cross; Cross-o'-th'-Moor; the two ladies of Bagstones and their antiquarian treasures; discovery of sepulchral urn by Mr Sainter, 1871; relics of battles between Romans and Britons; probable Roman encampment at Wincle; death of a poacher in Otter's Pool, 1868; otters and polecats nearly extinct but poaching prevalent; Wincle church; graveyard robbing; rush bearing; parish clerk buries a 'little 'un'; Wincle school.

White-lee Farm, or *Whitels,* as it is called in an agreement between the monks of Delacresse and the monks of Crokeden, when it was settled that its mill near Gig-hall, turned by the waters of the river Dane, should be exempted from tithes (*Dugdale*), joins *Wincle Grange*, both part of Swythamley, but on the Cheshire side of the Dane. In October, 1853, it was visited by a learned body of Rosicrucians, the brotherhood subsequently holding a chapter, when the following interesting account of Wincle Grange was read:-

HISTORY OF WINCLE GRANGE

Wincle Grange, a building of the red sandstone, or rather grit, situate on the high ground above Wincle, a township in the parish of Prestbury, was formerly erected by the monks of Combermere, near Nantwich. The house is a very interesting specimen of domestic architecture, with every appearance of bearing date about 1400, the details furnishing an example of transition from the decorated to the perpendicular style of gothic architecture. Wincle was a manor belonging to Hugh de Malbanc, who founded the Abbey of Combermere, and was the son of the Norman grantee of the barony of Wich Milbank. The manor is not only made mention of in the original charter of the abbey, but is referred to in the Taxation of Pope Nicholas, as follows:-"Item habet apud Wynkehall, in dec. de Maclesfild duas caruc. terr. et val. car. per annum, 10s." In the Valor Eccles, temp. Henry VIII there is the following: - "Reddit 'resolut' d'no regi lib'tatibz de Wyncall, 13s. 4d." In the 33rd Henry VIII the monastery, together with other lands, "Wincell Grange, Co. Cest." included, were granted to George Cotton, Esq. The present appearance of the Grange is in some respects different from what it originally was, but the main part of the building is not greatly altered. The walls are of considerable thickness. The house and buildings were probably little altered before the year 1670, when some possessor, whose initials are cut in stone over a stable door, appears to have mutilated it exceedingly, and given the premises their present look. At the same time, or perhaps yet more recently, the back parts of the dwelling house were pulled down, and the present kitchen, &c., built in place of the original building; the front and one side remain pretty much intact, and may furnish a pretty accurate idea of what it has once been. It is a house two storeys high, with a third series of rooms in the slope of the roof, so that, perhaps, it may be termed a three-storey house. The windows are all square-headed, and there are nine of them that yet remain more or less intact. The lowest to the front has above it an embattled moulding. It is of four lights, the mullions being what are termed hollow chamfers - the summits trefoiled and rather round. Between the interstices above the trefoiled heads are smaller and more angulated trefoils. This window has been altered at the left corner, and a perpendicular mullion introduced in place of the transition one. The centre window has had the original mullion removed, and plain chamfers inserted. The label above commences at the right hand corner with two quatrefoils set in squares, and followed with a wide and rather slender zig-zag ornament, of an unusual character. This window is three-lighted. The highest window has no label, is three-lighted, and similar in tracery to that on the ground floor. The wall on the inner, or north-west side, has been destroyed quite through the middle, so that only two windows, one above the other, are to be seen. They have been very near copies of the two lower ones of the front or gable end of the Grange, the first having the embattled ornament still existing, but all the rest replaced by much more modern work, that has a Jacobean look. The upper window is only in part left, and displays the zig-zag tracery and quatrefoil on its label. The north-east side has four windows, two above and two below. The wall is not in an unbroken line, but partly recessed. These windows are identical, in shape and detail, with the highest of the gable east, viz.: three-lighted with trefoiled heads, &c., and hollow chamfered mullions. The string course on the gable roof is terminated with a fleur-de-lis kind of trefoil. There is no one feature of antiquarian interest in the house. Within the yard of the north-east side stands a cross, identical in design with those of Clulow and Upton. This cross stands six feet out of the ground, and is ornamented with the double fillet, as are the others; the summit being squared and scalloped. The farm buildings on the north-west side of the Grange form altogether three sides of a square. The far side of what is now a stable, standing opposite the grange, is provided with buttresses; and I am informed that a piscina yet exists in the interior, but it was covered up with hay, and so not visible. The remainder of this building is all of the same character, and of the same date, as the one at the end of the yard. This, therefore, may be accounted an interesting example of an abbey grange, standing at a remote distance from the parent institution, on high and what were, for the most part, barren moorlands, overlooking the "Roaches," and about six or seven miles distant from Leek, in Staffordshire, quite on the verge of the county of Cheshire. In drawing an inference as to its date, the window tracery, mouldings and embattled ornaments are the only certain clues; and as these all correspond to the transition period, there can be no very good reasons for doubting that the erection took place some time between the years 1380 and 1420; whilst, as no former remains are left, we are led to the conclusion that either this Grange is the original one, or that the former building was entirely demolished at the time when the present one was constructed. The cross in the yard to the northeast has a much earlier look, and seems to point to an earlier edifice of a more unpretending character, but on this point I prefer for the present to remain silent. That the value of the manor was gradually increasing through cultivation appears plain, seeing that in the reign of Edward I it was taxed at 10s., and in that of Henry VIII at 13s. 4d.

In 1762, by a marriage with the Trafford and Stonehewer families, the estate of *Barleighford* became entirely attached to Swythamley. It borders on the White-lea and Wincle Grange farms, the house being situated amongst hanging woods and in the midst of beautiful and varied scenery, through which winds the turbulent river Dane. Part of the building is of remote date; some of the ceilings and fireplaces are curious and uncommon, the panellings and carving showing evidence of having been executed at different periods. Within the memory of individuals now living, a fine herony existed there; but, unfortunately, many of the old oaks were felled, causing the herons to desert, and establish a fresh herony at a distance, where the noble birds can rest secure from such ruthless desecration and destruction of their ancient homes.

The *Bridestones* stand about one hundred yards north of the roads running from Rushton to Congleton, two miles from the Rushton railway station. This remarkable relic consists of several large unhewn freestones, a number of which are arranged in the form of a parallelogram eighteen feet long by eleven wide.

The height of the side stones averages about five and a half feet above ground, and in thickness from one to three feet. It is probable they were formerly covered horizontally. The parallelogram stands due east and west; and the whole of its side formerly, consisted of one large stone eighteen feet long, weighing not less than ten tons. Close to the S. E. corner stands a large and erect pillar, rising about nine and a half feet in height. Another and smaller obelisk six feet high is situated five yards from the N. E. corner.

The Rev T. Harwood, D.D., F.S.A., considered this place as the remains of an ancient *cave,* whilst by others the remains of a *cist-vaen.*

The *Archæologia,* Vol. II. xli, mentions one similar in Stansfield, Yorkshire, bearing the same name. Mr Ward, in his "Stoke-on-Trent," thinks these remains are sacrificial altars, which were also used as tombs for the chief Druids. Bones have been found in the one at Rushton.

There is a remarkable hill, covered with trees, about two miles from Swythamley, on the Macclesfield road, called *Clulow Cross.* On the summit, buried in the wood, is the upright pillar of an old cross, where it is said the country people from the district in the time of the great plague brought and left the produce of their farms, for the townspeople to fetch, so as to avoid crossing the infected boundary. In Sutton, distance two or three miles nearer Macclesfield, on the edge of Wild-Boar Clough, is an upright, broad, flat stone, having a cross within a circle at the top, and called *"Cross-o'-th'-moor."* Possibly both stones were "mere-stones" placed by the monks of the Abbey of Combermere. Not far from Clulow Cross, two worthy ladies, famed for their travels and researches amongst objects of antiquity and interest in distant parts of the world, have built a charmingly-situated summer residence at the verge of a pine wood overlooking the picturesque valley of the river Dane; where from their windows they enjoy one of the most lovely views our mountain country affords.

> "Oh scene of beauty, all unpraised, unknown;
> By fluent pen, nor glowing canvas shown ! -
> The rugged precipice, the smiling vale;
> The golden woods; the hill, the rock, the dale;
> Hamlet and cottage, bridge and country. - All
> Blended in one sweet picture."

The place is known by the name of *Bakstone,* from tradition that, in earlier times, *bake-stones,* called by the country folk *bak-stones* (used for baking old-cake), were procured from a quarry in the wood behind the house. Others call it *Bagston, bagg* in certain dialects meaning *badger (Meles taxus),* which rare British quadruped is yet found in the stony and rocky parts of the adjacent woods. It is also the old family crest of the owner of Bagston. Near the Bagston wood is a remarkably fine oak, the trunk of the tree measuring more than twenty feet in circumference. The house contains many curious and valuable relics, collected during the journeyings of the ladies in far-off Eastern lands, and in the collection are a few antiquarian treasures, obtained by themselves in their own immediate neighbourhood. Among these, worthy of notice, are the fragments of an urn, found in the midst of a singular ring of stones near Clulow Cross, known by the name of the *Bullstrang.* The *Macclesfield Courier*, of September, 1871, thus describes the discovery:-

"ARCHÆOLOGY - In a field behind Clulow Cross, in Wincle, there is to be seen a stone circle, about five yards in diameter, with a broad, upright slab of gritstone placed in the centre. On Wednesday last an excavation was made on the southern aspect of the slab, in the presence of Mr Sainter (the well-known archæologist) and others. About three feet from the surface there were discovered bits of charcoal, along with stone, blackened by fire, and a sepulchral urn, which contained the burnt bones of a young child, also a piece of curved flint that had been calcined and possibly used as the sacrificial knife. The urn, made of baked clay, proved to be in a crumbling condition, but two or three larger portions were preserved, and as there was an ornamentation to be seen in the outer surfaces, the burial may be assigned to a very old date, probably prehistoric or anterior to the period of the occupation of this country by the Romans."

It is clear that the neighbourhood of Leek and Swythamley have been the scenes of battles between the Romans and Britons, from the fact of arms and relics of both nations having been found at various times. Dr Plott, in his "History of Staffordshire," 1686, observes: - "Nor did the Britons only head their arrows with flint, but also their *mataræ* or *British darts,* which were thrown by those that fought in *effedis,* or chariots, whereof I guess this is one I had given me, found near Leek by my worthy friend, Mr Thomas Gent, curiously jagged at the edges, with such like teeth as a sickle, and otherwise wrought upon the flat." A similar flint arrow-head, as described by Dr Plott in 1686, was discovered by Miss B - in 1872, around which was clinging the roots of a piece of heather she had brought from the Back Forest to plant at Bagston.

In removing a portion of the foundations of what had been the original site of the old Grange of Swythamley, a curious Ancient British *net-sinker* was brought to light. It is made of flint, and perforated, that a cord might pass through its centre. Near to where the stone net-sinker was found, and inside one of the rooms, an old *draw-well* existed which was in use during the memory of the writer. At Bartomley, a Swythamley farm on the Cheshire side of the river Dane, in Wincle township, have at various times been discovered a considerable number of Roman antiquities, consisting of gold rings, in one instance with a god or goddess engraved on the jewel, gold chains, with links of curious green stone called *prez,* together with gold ornaments; considered by Mr Meyer, the well-known antiquarian of Liverpool, to be bosses or shield ornaments, the last discovery being a very beautiful fibula of virgin gold. These things have been usually picked up, after the plough has disturbed the soil, on a steep bank resembling artificial earthworks, probably a Roman encampment, and at the foot of which, through a wooded ravine, flows the Dane.

Near to this spot, a pretty waterfall tumbles, splashing and sparkling, into the river, where a deep, dark pool is formed, called the "otters' pool," out of which, and surrounded by dense foliage, rises, almost perpendicular from the water, a grey, moss grown rock. Here occurred in June, 1868, a fatal accident. Tempted by the clearness of the water, a young man, and a noted poacher, had sprung from the summit of the rock, with the intention of diving, but in the performance of the feat, a projecting stone came in contact with his skull, rendering him, it is presumed, insensible; as a friend of the writer's, accompanied by a gamekeeper named James Barber, who has filled that office for nearly forty years on the estate, in the act of throwing a fly round a corner of the rock, perceived something white lying glistening at the bottom of the pool, which ultimately proved to be the dead and naked body of the unfortunate poacher.

Otters are now rarely, if ever, seen on this part of the river, as a deadly feud has long existed between this silent trout-stealer and the keepers. A pack of otter-hounds, the property of Lord Hill, come occasionally to hunt within a few miles, but chiefly in the neighbourhood of the large meres found in Cheshire. The polecat is also another nearly extinct animal, though at one period a very common depredator in the district. The game is, however, by no means safe by the wholesale destruction of its four-legged foes, as large gangs of determined men, numbering from eighteen to twenty in a gang, have frequent and desperate encounters with the game-watchers and their powerful night dogs.

Wincle *Church* is a fabric of stone, with a low, castellated tower. The present building has been erected upwards of a century, but the original chapel was built in the time of Charles I, and was described by Gastrell, in 1717, as "a very handsome one." It had, however, neither pulpit, communion-table nor font; but there was a reading desk at the upper end. Children had been baptized, but "no sacrament administered." According to tradition, the churchyard had been licensed for burials by Bishop Hall. The same tradition saith, that a

Wincle Grange

Bagstones

'Rest and Welcome', Bagstones

Roman Antiquities

Otter's Pool

Wincle Church and School

Fishing on the Dane

certain hospital at Manchester procured the greater portion of its anatomical subjects from this churchyard, through the means of the sexton being bribed to sell the bodies, which were conveyed away the same night of the burial. The minister had no stated salary, the people paying what they pleased for preaching, "when there was any, but there had been none for half a year past," in 1717. (Geo. Ormerod, LL.D., F.R.S., F.S.A.)

Over the door of the church, cut in stone, are the words:-
"Here doe O Lord svre plant Thy Word. Wincle Ch."

Until a comparatively recent period, the floor of Wincle Church was neither paved nor flagged, but spread with *rushes*. These were renewed annually, on a certain Sunday in July, when it was usual to decorate a cart with flowers and bear them to the church. This was celebrated with great rejoicing, and was termed the *rush-bearing;* and in after years, when rushes were no longer employed, the drinking and name was still kept up.

Another tradition, not yet quite faded away, is that of the old parish clerk there, who, in the absence of a clergyman, himself "buried" a child. He had looked many times up Wincle hill to see if the expected clergyman from Maxfelt was in sight, but had looked in vain. What was to be done? The sun was getting low, the mourners becoming impatient, so he "just slipped on the surplice," and read the service, justifying himself afterwards for what he had done, by saying that "after all it was but a *little 'un.*"

The prettiness and picturesqueness of the school and school-house at Wincle, makes up to some extent for the primitive plainness of the church. The school was built and endowed a few years since, at the cost of the late Mrs Thomas Daintry, of North Rode, Cheshire; it is an ornament to the little village, and it is to be sincerely hoped that the rising generation of young agriculturists who are there receiving a sound education, will grow up into manhood with more liberal ideas and less penurious habits than their predecessors.

MISCELLANIA

The loss of the 'Swythamley'; a woman with 107 grandchildren, Leekfrith; visit of steam carriage to Swythamley, 1868; death of Richard Hassall, sculptor, 1868; improvement of the local roads by Mr Brocklehurst; rebuilding of the bridge at Danebridge.

As a compliment to the old squire, an intimate friend and fellow sportsman, and a large shipowner of Liverpool, christened one of his ships the *Swythamley;* but the sailors, confused with the name, called her the *Sweetemily.* The vessel was ultimately unfortunate, for in a Liverpool paper, dated September 30th, 1862, appeared the following paragraph:-

"LOSS OF AN INDIAMAN, COTTON LADEN - Intelligence has been received in Liverpool, by the Cape mail, of the total loss of the Liverpool ship *Swythamley,* bound from Bombay to Liverpool. The vessel was lost on the Blenheim reef, near the Cape. The crew were saved, but the cargo was lost. It comprised 2,976 bales of cotton. The *Swythamley* left Liverpool for Kurrachee on the last day of August, 1861. She was owned by Messrs. Moore & Co., and was classed A1 for 12 years. It is a somewhat singular coincidence that the *American,* which left Bombay on the same day as the *Swythamley,* has also been lost."

In the obituary of a Leek paper we find:-

"On the 25th ult., aged 102, Mrs Elizabeth Mills, of Leek-frith, Swythamley. She was the mother of 11 children, grandmother to 44, and great-grandmother to 107. This venerable old lady was remarkably active to the latter end of her days, frequently visiting her neighbours, and assisting in their domestic duties. During the last harvest she assisted her son (a stout lad of 80) in haymaking."

A few years before her death, the *boy,* as she called her son, fell ill for a few days, when she expressed her fear that he was delicate, and that she doubted whether she would be able to *rear* him.

In the *Macclesfield Courier* of July 1868, was the following description of what may possibly be our future mode of travelling:-

"A DARING EXPLOIT. - On Monday last, an extraordinary looking carriage, propelled entirely by steam power, and containing a large party of gentlemen well known to the scientific world, was seen slowly climbing, and with equal sureness and safety, quietly descending the frightfully precipitous and dangerous stony hills that lie between Macclesfield and the valley of the Dane, in Wincle. Ascending from there, the gradient is steeper and more difficult than any to be found on the wonderful Mount Cenis line of rail. Yet the grey-looking monster toiled up, apparently with little effort, and from the summit dashed away at full speed to Swythamley Park, where Mr Philip Brocklehurst hospitably entertained the passengers at lunch. A countryman, living at the Old Smithy farm, had, a few days previously, confessed to having seen in his dreams a nondescript fiery wagon, without horses, clambering up the almost impassable hills near his house, and, when working in his hay on Monday, the reality suddenly rushed past, its startling effect on his nervous system can be easier imagined than described. The homeward journey of the adventurous party was equally fortuitous. Thanks to the consummate skill and nerve displayed by the two gentlemen acting as driver and stoker, the trip was from first to last an entire success, and probably unparalleled in the history of road-steam locomotion."

In the same journal, dated July 18th, 1868, we read of the loss of a promising young sculptor, originating from Swythamley, one of whose earliest efforts is a clever representation of a toad carved in stone, and preserved in the cave at Rock Hall.

"RICHARD P. HASSALL, SCULPTOR. - Death has this week deprived Macclesfield of a genius. Born and reared at Pheasant Clough farm, the Roaches (Leek frith), the peaceful pursuit of agriculture was his youthful uncongenial occupation. Robust and powerful in body, and with a mind ardent, healthy and teeming with ideas of the most poetic kind, Richard Hassall, at the age of 25, entered the Macclesfield School of Art to perfect himself in that which has cost him his life. Studying late and early (often commencing at the school at half-past three in the summer morning), he made great progress; but the all-engrossing love of art led to neglect of physical nourishment, and indifferent health resulted. Thus four or five years were spent in successfully accomplishing everything he undertook, gaining medals, national medallions, Queen's prizes, becoming a free student, and ultimately an art pupil teacher. Leaving the school at thirty, for two years he devoted himself to wood-carving, stone-cutting and sculpture. But Macclesfield had a poor appreciation for such business, and insufficient patronage drove him nearly to the verge of despair. Yet he was thankful that Mr Brocklehurst, of Swythamley Hall, had introduced him to see and study the few Grecian wonders in the Macclesfield Institution. Whilst at his father's farm, the chisel was his delight. Thirty or forty heads, arranged around the walls of the barn, startled and pleased Mr Brocklehurst. They were bought by him, and soon after the youthful sculptor was here learning the rudiments of art. Two years and a half ago, the head designer and sculptor of the South Kensington Museum died - a young man of great promise - and Mr Hassall was sent for. There he gained the respect and esteem of all who knew him, and his productions were considered of great promise. Earnest was the purpose of Mr Hassall's life, and to that one purpose he was wholly devoted. Though his career was short, it was yet bright and full of worthy works. They speak for themselves. He was original in thought, and belonged to that class of men having a superabundance of feeling and of fancy, that power of

Richard Hassall

Old Bridge, Danebridge

New Bridge, Danebridge

The Weir below Whitelee

suggestion and combination which raised him above mere imitation, or following in the steps of those who had gone before him. But why dwell upon one whose like in this county has never been met, except in the late Mr Gatley? To see his productions - (there are a few in this town) - is to see the touch of a delicate hand, a refined mind, a vigorous will, and whom to have known intimately was a great pleasure."

Up to 1860, and previous to Mr Brocklehurst renovating Swythamley and making it his residence, the roads in the neighbourhood were only suitable for strongly-built carts or travellers on horseback, and more resembled a Spanish mule-track than an English highway; they were narrow, badly kept and dangerous; the country folk and farmers, from the old-fashioned method of conveying their buxom wives and daughters on *pillions* behind them on horseback, cared little for their rugged and miry condition. Between Wincle and Macclesfield two impetuous streams had to be forded, a rather hazardous proceeding on a dark tempestuous winter night, as on one occasion the late squire, riding home in the evening to Tytherington Hall, his Cheshire seat, from a shooting expedition to Swythamley, while endeavouring to swim his hack across the swollen current near Sutton Hall (the ancient house of the Earls of Lucan), was drawn under water, and narrowly escaped drowning. All this has been happily changed; handsome stone bridges span the streams, hedges have been levelled, the highways widened, and the bucolic damsels of the district, no longer satisfied with jogging to "Maxfelt tine" on the broad fat back of the market "tit," the leathern belt of the "sarvant mon" in front firmly grasped with the hand unoccupied by the *butter and egg* basket, now may be seen riding in a conveyance on springs and wheels, resplendent with sticky varnish and bright green paint, often the handiwork of a native artist. In 1860 Mr Brocklehurst commenced his efforts to establish a daily post through the country, and was at last successful by becoming the guarantee to Government for any loss that might accrue from the undertaking. For several years he was mulcted to a considerable amount, but now the post is not only self-supporting but profitable. In those dark days, if a letter by chance was intended to penetrate this then forsaken and neglected district, it might have waited for weeks in some roadside public before the owner even *heard* of it, probably too late to be of any service. The common excuse made by the inhabitants for being a century behind their neighbours beyond the mountains was, "theer fo'-faythers did'ner mither theer breens, an' new fangl't nowtions wer'ner allais so reet as t'odens."

The last bridge erected was over the river Dane, in Wincle - a fine, single arch and at a considerable height above the water. The counties of Staffordshire and Cheshire each granted £1,000, Mr Brocklehurst giving the land and material, and assisting at the work to about the same amount; he also, at the request of the builders and other friends, undertook, on August 11th, 1869, to lay the first springer-stone, on which occasion a handsome silver-mounted mallet, bearing a suitable inscription, was presented to him; after which the party partook of luncheon at the Hall, and arrangements were made for the workpeople to drink success to the new link connecting the two counties of Staffordshire and Cheshire. In pulling down the old narrow bridge, which, though picturesque, had become very unsafe, a cannon ball, beaten with hammers into a spherical form (not cast in a mould, as in the present day), was was discovered - a supposed relic left by a portion of Cromwell's army, when moving across country, in 1645, on its way to attack Biddulph Castle, near Congleton.

Among the rubble of the old bridge was found a silver shilling of Charles I, struck in 1644, at the commencement of the civil war. "It is in fine preservation, and the legend on the reverse refers to the declaration with which Charles determined to resist the Parliament:-

> REL[igio] PROT [ecta].
> LEG[is] ANG [liæ].
> LIB [ertas] PAR [liamenti].
> 1644.

"The Prince of Wales feathers may show that the coin was struck at Bristol, but this is not quite certain." - *W.T.W. Vaux* (Keeper of the coins in the British Museum).

The bridge fell unexpectedly during its removal, carrying with it eight men into the river, several of them being seriously injured by the fall.

There is yet much left to be recorded of this interesting but little-known part of the country; and the many valuable MSS and documents, now in careful keeping at Stafford, which were generously bequeathed by the late Mr Salt to his native county, will doubtless some day yield much ancient lore and history that has long been hidden away.

APPENDIX 1

'Notes on a portion of the Northern Borders of Staffordshire'
by William Beresford
*(extracts from a series of articles published in
The Reliquary between July 1863 and October 1866)*

1

The origin of the Bridestones - a local legend

The peasants of the neighbourhood have a curious legend respecting the origin of "The Bridestones." "When the Danes invaded England," say they, "a Danish youth became enamoured of a Saxon lady, and in the end the two were married at Biddulph Church (about a mile and a half distant); but on returning from the wedding, they were here met and murdered, and after their interment had taken place in the spot where they fell, these stones were laid round their grave, and the name *Bridestones* given to it from that circumstance." So much for popular opinion.

2

Seventeenth century inscriptions at Fenton Farm

I have yet another interesting place to notice before we have done with Buglawton, and that also is situated on the borders of the township, about two miles N. of the Bridestones, two and a half N.E. of Congleton, and one N.W. of the Railway station at Bosley. The curiosity to which I allude is to be found at the Farm of *Fenton,* belonging to John Antrobus, Esq. The house is a dilapidated building of the Elizabethan period, having at present only the body of the building and one wing entire. The "front door," a broad and massive one, is thickly studded with square nail heads, and opened by means of a large iron ring. On the occasion of my last visit (June, 1863), my knock was answered by a clean and homely looking farmer's wife, who kindly proceeded to show me the curious inscriptions of which I had heard so much, and which were to be found, I understood, in a chamber of her house. Before mounting the old fashioned oaken stairs, I noticed a small room which had some time been wainscoted to the ceiling, but its walls are now bare with the exception of a few places still covered by the relics of oaken panelling. Here also was an old chair of the same material close to a chest equally ancient, in which, Mrs. Lomas informed me, her landlord takes great interest. Finding, however, nothing remarkable about them, we passed up the stairs, and came to a room oblong in form, and about six yards by four in size. All the windows had been walled up - a few panes of glass inserted by the present occupants admitting the only light. By the aid of a candle, however, I was enabled to examine the place more closely, and found the walls to be adorned with illuminations, inscriptions, &c. We entered by a door at the extremity of the southern side, and this is the wall I will first notice. It has been divided into semicircles, oblongs, &c., by the painter drawing upon it broad black lines in imitation of beams. Along the top, near the ceiling, ran three oblongs or panels, in which the following inscriptions had been neatly painted in old fashioned Roman capitals :—

(I) "So live as thy end (II) "Lov thy neighbor (III) "Doe to all men as

　　Bee not ferefull."　　　As thyselfe alway."　　Thov wovld be dv: vn"—

The parts of each panel unoccupied by the letters were filled up by neat floral designs, each of the three differing in pattern. In a large oblong under the first inscription were the following four lines, (two being in old Roman capitals, and the other two in old English black letter characters):-

　　"In my beginge, God be My Good spide; Grace and vertue
　　longe to proceede me. Hericy Smith, alies Gilder, I629."

> "Do nothing but to good advise: take counsell of ye wise,
> So yt the cloudes of ignorance shall be banish fro thine eyes."

Under inscription No. II there is a partly illegible verse on the value of a true friend; and under the third, also in black letter, stand these lines:-

> "The compiny of him that's wyse, although hee bee but poore,
> Is Better then the foole that's riche who layes up craft in store.
> Spar not to spend thy golde & wealth for meat, for drink, for cloth,
> For wisdome, lerneinge, and for health, or else to spende be loth."

The west *end* of the room seems to have been occupied by a window, or partially covered by the head of a bed, and consequently no inscriptions are found there. The side wall opposite to the door by which we entered bears upon it four verses, one of which appears to say that the *wife,* and not the "onely childe," should be intrusted with secrets, but generally speaking, the rest, being upon the outside wall, are so much injured by damp and old age, as to be almost illegible. The eastern end also bears inscriptions, floral work, and verses, all much defaced. One of the latter seems to run as follows:-

> "Before thou sleep, call to thy mind what thou hast done that day,
> and if thy consience be opprest, to God for mercy pray,
> Leade such a life that still thy soule may stand in state of joy,
> Although the world a thousand waies thy consience doe anoy."

The only colour employed appears to have been *black;* although as the artist was a *gilder,* other colours and even *gold* may have been used. The whole work from beginning to end was beautifully executed, and especially the floral designs on the higher portions of the walls.

The body of the room is chiefly occupied by three corn bins &c., put up by the present tenants of the farm - the family of Lomas - who have been here for several generations. The partitions between the bins are composed of oak, giving to the place the appearance of a small chapel, indeed, by some it has been considered as such, and the inscriptions (which they were unable to decipher) were by them affirmed to be "The Lord's Prayer and Ten Commandments in *Latin, Greek, and another language or two* !" Such the honest farmer's wife informed me they were before I saw them, having received her information from some persons or other who had been to inspect them. I consider the room, however, as nothing more than the bedroom of a former owner and occupant of the place, who built up the windows in order to give uniformity and additional effect to the painting on the walls when seen by candlelight; or it may, perhaps, have been occupied by some secluded Catholic, during the times of persecution, and the fourth line of the inscription last quoted seems to corroborate this idea. But, be that as it may, the place is certainly very interesting, as illustrating the tastes and ideas of at least *one* of our forefathers, and as shewing that the land was not so deeply sunk in vice and immorality during the reign of the unfortunate Charles I as some have imagined.

3

Bosley customs

The VILLAGE of Bosley presents no features of especial interest. Two plain whitewashed cottages, built in the last century, on the northern side of the church, were formerly occupied as the *Parsonage.* But in 1853, the present Incumbent, the Rev W. Sutcliffe, M.A., caused a new and handsome residence of brick to be erected on its south-western side; and to his praiseworthy exertions are mainly owing the beautiful new schools, the chancel of the church, and many other improvements.

Amongst old customs, the practice of begging *soul cake* is still celebrated at Bosley, together with the last faint trace of the ancient "*mysteries,*" "*miracle plays,*" &c. The play chiefly enacted is that of "St George and the Turk," derived originally, I presume, from the fabled story of the Crusaders at Antioch receiving supernatural aid from heaven, against their Saracen opponents; when at the head of his great white army, St George descended, and as the *Troubadours* sang, put the infidels to rout -

> "A blood red crosse was on his arm,
> A dragon on his breaste;
> A little garter all of golde,
> Was round his leg exprest."

Another ancient, as well as useful and pleasant custom, has been lately revived at Bosley, by the Rev W. Sutcliffe - I mean the ringing of the *Curfew* bell. It is *useful*, because it declares the time to the villagers around; and it is *pleasant*, because it conjures up the remembrance of bitter scenes of tyranny, only that we may know they are now no more; and that as we gaze on the cheerful fire no longer extinguished on our hearths at night, we may in fancy rove back o'er the past, and profitably compare the dark state of our country's infancy with the full bloom of her present happiness.

4

Around Three Shires Head

If we go into Wildboarclough, and there, seated in the "chimney-corner" of some old farmhouse, ask one of its "ancient men" for a tale of the olden time, he will most probably relate only a ghost story, and tell how "Winca' parson" once *bottled up* an apparition; and by burying her deep in the churchyard, "laid" her, "an' whoo nevver coom noo moor." We will therefore leave the clough, and make our way to "Panniers' Pool Bridge," where the road leads us out of Cheshire into Derbyshire, and immediately again into Staffordshire. This is, in fact, the place where the three counties meet, and a wild one indeed it is. We leave Cheshire by an old stone bridge which crosses the Dane, called *Panniers'* Bridge, because it was once only sufficiently wide for a packhorse carrying *panniers* to cross it. It has, however, been widened. Several yards lower down the stream, the brook which divides Derbyshire from Staffordshire, enters the Dane at *Panniers' Pool,* and brings down a flood of coloured mineral water, leaving on the stones over which it passes, a thick sediment of yellow ochre. It rises chiefly in an old coalpit shaft about a mile distant, and near the "Penny-hole" pits. It will be found elaborately described in Mr Wardle's Geological Chapter appended to Mr Sleigh's "History of Leek." Some superstitious folks in the neighbourhood prize this water as being a cure for *witchcraft;* and sagely consider that a draught of it for nine mornings in succession is necessary to effect a cure. I need only say, that this notion is there received as *truth,* and I give to every thinking mind an ample index both to the place and many of its inhabitants.

A wilder and more thoroughly "Moorland" spot than *Panniers Pool,* situated at the junction of Cheshire, Derbyshire, and Staffordshire, could scarcely be imagined. Environed by bold and lofty hills, traversed only by a few passengers, and perpetually echoing with the murmur of falling water, the place almost seems to retain the solitude which it must have enjoyed in the earliest years. The bounding deer, the merry pack-horse train, and the sturdy buttoneers no longer cross its streams, or fill its limpid waters with gay reflections. Even the "three shire stone," which stood on the Derbyshire side, bearing "H" (the initial of *Hartington*), has been removed, and nothing save the name now remains, - the name marked on the maps of Plott, Drayton, and other topographers equally ancient.

Crossing over Pannier's Bridge, the tourist pursues the road running by the brook which enters Dane at the shire heads, and separates for a short distance the counties of Derby and Stafford. As he ascends the stream the water gradually deepens in colour until it changes from a light to a reddish yellow. He passes the mouths of several old coal pits and here and there sees seams of the glossy mineral creeping out by the brook side. A little higher he arrives at the place where the coloured stream runs out of a tunnel made to admit air to the "Penny Hole" coal pits, and to take the water from them. The country people call it *alum water* from its peculiar taste; but analysis proves it to be largely impregnated with peroxide of iron. Its petrifying qualities are also so strong that "any small organism" placed in it becomes changed into a stonelike body in twenty-four hours - (*Staffordshire Advertiser*, November 1, 1862). Some of the gentlemen who have analysed this water remark that *ironstone* of even a valuable kind might be discovered in the neighbourhood. It seems, however, that the metal has been already found and worked, for, near a rock, no great distance from Penny Hole, there was once a forge for beating the rude metal, and, I believe, also a place for smelting the stone, but the man who carried on the business, together with the buildings in which he worked have long since become things of the past. Hence a little anecdote respecting him may not be out of place in the "RELIQUARY." He was, it seems, an enterprising and thrifty man and possessed of wit as keen as the wintry blasts of his native hills. One day he went to Swithamley Hall, and asked Squire Trafford's permission to cut a "hammer *steal* "[1] in the woods. The squire wondered at so small a request; and telling him that he might have cut one without asking, gave him leave to do so anywhere. The forgeman thanked him, went his way, and cut down the best *tree* he could find on the estate; still it was only a "hammer stail"[2] and, as the permission had been given, the irate squire discovered the magnitude of *forge hammers* a little too late. "The Forge," as the rock is still called, is situated about the middle of an imaginary line, drawn from Flash to Pannier's Pool. A little lower down the same glen are the ruins of an old hut called Hake's neest[3] (Hawk's nest).

We are now in the vicinity of *Flash,* in the place where, years ago, dwelt the noted "*Flashmen*". It is a wild and barren place, - heath stone walls, and black commons, meet the eye on every side, and there is scarcely a tree to be seen for miles. One stands in a perfect labyrinth of hills, with deep and narrow valleys running in almost every direction. The cottages on these dreary moors are generally as ugly and as low as possible, and seem hugging the ground to avoid the winds. Still, I think you will generally find a white apron and a clean floor, a bright fire, and smiling faces, in most of them. Colliers are the usual occupants, and as most people are aware, a collier likes a "snuggery," but, as he can lie in a little compass, and does not require a large house, these huts, small though they may be, are adapted to the wants of their inhabitants.

5
Collieries of the Upper Dane valley

A considerable number of coalpits exist in this vicinity; and all of them lie within a few miles of Flash, which is about five miles S.W. from Buxton, and seven miles N. by E. from Leek. The coal is generally small, and not of the best quality. I append a list of them, in order of their age, italicising those now working, and sometimes adding in figures the number of yards from their mouths to the ends of their tunnels. These mines, it must be remembered, are generally levels, driven horizontally into the hill sides, so that the coal can be brought out on small tramways.

1. - MACCLESFIELD FOREST, CHESHIRE

1. Dane, 900 yards.
2. Greenhills, old workings 600 to 700 yards; later, 400 to 500 yards.
3. Dane Thorne, 200 yards out of *Dane.*
4. *Robinsclough,* 400 yards, and older workings for 150 yards further.[4]

11 - DERBYSHIRE

1. Blackclough, $\frac{1}{4}$ mile. Coals used to be *boated* out of this pit on a canal. There is a road out of it into Dane, and the men of the two collieries used sometimes to meet underground and smoke their pipes together.

2. Wooden Spoon, $\frac{1}{2}$ mile from commencement of Pennyhole.

3. *Crash-away, or Moss Pit*: has a shaft and engine. Water taken by Burbage level which runs up from Burbage near Buxton.

4. *Back o'th' Moss,* with a tunnel for conveying coal to the High Peak Railway.

III. - STAFFORDSHIRE

1. *Goldsich.* Shaft.   3. Diamond Hill.
2. Hazelburrow.   4. *Blue Hills.* Shaft.
5. *Pennyhole.* 200 to 300 yards. Communication with Wooden Spoon, the water from which ran down by this level. Air-tunnel 600 to 800 yards out of which runs the mineral water.

Many disheartening difficulties are necessarily experienced in working these pits. The seams of coal are thin and poor, and broken by many "*faults;*" and the mineral itself is generally of a dull colour. But the greatest obstacle in the way of working them is the want of a *railway* through the district to convey the coal to other parts, and so make the trade remunerative.

6

Industry and character in Flash and the Moorlands

It is now, it seems, more than two hundred years since the coal trade and the button manufacture were introduced into this wild country. Intimately connected with the latter, as pedestrian hawkers, were the noted "Flash men," living in the last century, and already mentioned. They squatted on the moors about Flash, and made it their business to carry buttons over the country, for sale. Travelling from town to town, and speaking a sort of cant, or slang dialect, they soon obtained their peculiar name, and became notorious for their rude, half savage manners, and brutal pastimes. Increasing in numbers, they became a nuisance to the vicinity, and it was then resolved to eject them; but no bailiff could, for a while, be found sufficiently bold for the purpose. When, however, an officer was procured who undertook to arrest several of them, other landlords followed the example of the prime mover: they who refused to become tenants left the district and formed the "Broken Cross Gang," whilst the more peaceably disposed consented to settle down in the cultivation of farms, and some of their descendants remain on the spot to the present day.

Button making early formed a great feature of the industry of this neighbourhood, and continued such until some years had elapsed in the present century. Small round moulds of wood were dyed of a darker colour in some of the mineral springs about Flash,[5] and then covered with cloth. The stitches which held the covering on the mould crossed each other at the centre of the back, and so formed a *shank*. Very different, therefore, were these rude buttons from the patent beauties of 1864.

I have a few by me now, given to me by a former maker, who assures me that the manufacture was, at one time, a source of livelihood to her neighbours on the moorlands; the pay[6] being 16d. to 20d. for making a bag of 24 doz. small or vest buttons, and 4s. to 4s. 6d. for a bag of 12 doz. larger or coat buttons. The females at almost every house carried it on, and so were able to support their "lords" in a state of comparative idleness. Thus the latter, caring little for the pick, the spade, or the plough, sometimes assisted their wives with the buttons, and sometimes turned themselves into "public characters," procured steeds, hung collars of tinkling bells around their necks, and, mounting packs of buttons and twist, set off on their hawking expeditions through the country. Those were prosperous days for the Northern Borderers. The shining face of many a homely matron brightened into a smile as she rocked the cradle with her foot, and watched the buttons in her white apron grow swiftly more under her glancing needle. And the golden guineas chinked merrily in many an old stocking[7] drawn from the thatch of many a cot now roofless, and from under the hearth-flag of many a home that has long been desolate.

As a specimen of the industry of those times may be mentioned the fact, that by five o'clock A.M. the women were often seen crowding to Flash for supplies of grocery goods. But there came a change. The introduction of machinery into the button trade took it away from the district, although the women there ascribe its departure to the conduct of two men at Flash, who are said to have purchased old clothes and cloth, and cut them up into lengths for overlaying the moulds; and thus by covering the buttons with an inferior material they were able to reduce both the quality and the price of the goods. This was doubtless a great agent in ruining the trade, for the price for making was reduced to 3d. per bag, and the profit in selling from 10s. 6d. to 3s. But the women concerned did not allow the matter to pass off quietly. One of them had a lawsuit at Leek through a quarrel with the chief cheap-trader, whose shop was at Flash; and numbers of the stout dames raised a mob of *themselves* and marched to Biddulph Moor.

The Moorlanders of last century seem to have been a cool, hardy, and enterprising race. Besides the pack-horsemen, some embarked in the "Manchester trade," i.e. they purchased stocks of woollen and linen goods, chiefly clothes, and conveyed them in carts over many parts of Great Britain. Nevertheless they generally returned hither and ended their days within a short distance of either the Dane or the Dove. A grey-headed few of them still linger on, still smoke their pipes in the chimney corners, and now and then tell tales of their adventures, with all the pride of the returned veteran, who can;

> "Strip his sleeve to show his scars,"

or

> "Shoulder his crutch, and tell how fields are won."

No one should, therefore, be surprised if he heard an old Moorlander comparing the various merits of Berwick and Brighton, or telling of some similar adventures which he met with on the mountains of Merioneth, and the fens of Lincoln.

From these peregrinations they derive, I presume, the intelligence which characterizes the older inhabitants; and although they certainly have a few superstitions and prejudices inherent to their wild country, they are nevertheless a frugal, generous, and hospitable people, advanced beyond the condition in which I, as a stranger, expected to find them. Still some of the roguish pranks practised by young farmers nearer Leek, long years ago, yet linger here. Many young couples (and old ones too), on the morning of their marriage day, have been vexed (though not, perhaps, *surprised*) to find the wedding car *minus* a wheel;[8] and also on the first morning of the honeymoon, a happy bridegroom has often risen to find himself a prisoner in his own house; the door securely tied or chained on the *outside,* and every wall of the building firmly propped up by a miscellaneous collection of great *field gates.* And a prisoner has he had to remain, condoling himself on the kindly interest some young unknown took in the safety of his dwelling under the *tremendous* rejoicing expected to take place. Nor has he been liberated until a stray peasant, through the *merest chance,* of course, happens to pass the spot, and by a very circuitous process to set him free. Such is "life" on the most Northern Moorlands, and the people undoubtedly enjoy it.

But, though longer rambles may have ceased, the borderers are not always shut up at home. Years ago the good old farmer and his wife might have been seen jogging along to market on one cart horse, their heads nodding "time" to its measured trot, and their shoulders shooting right and left to agree with its motion. In our days, however, when the means of conveyance are so much improved, some come rambling into town in their trim "traps," and others in the good old-fashioned cart. But the poorest have yet to walk, and you may generally know these when you see them in town, by their jolly hardy faces, their low felt hats, the "smock frocks," the leggings, and their stout "ash plants".

But in point of intelligence and good manners, the wealthier farmers of the Moorlands fall behind few of their fellow-agriculturists in even more favoured situations. This being the case, it will be asked, "How, then, have the legendary stories of the district been originated and preserved?" The question seems easily answered, The stories existing here are not nearly so numerous as we generally suppose; and the greater part of them are such as are told by the lowest and most ignorant of the inhabitants, and such, too, as the older and more intelligent will neither repeat nor believe. The long and dreary winters, the biting winds and huge snow drifts of the district, which shut up the peasants by their turf fires, have, I think, had a great deal to do with fabricating the lower class of these legends. Every body knows that a dark night is the most productive of ghost stories, spiriting them forth from the dim and dingy caves of memory to appear but only on the hearth, to afright but only the credulous; and to prepare the imaginative minds of gossips to turn, as they go homeward in the dark, a donkey into a demon, and its kindly salute into the "shriek of a spirit lost." The Ghost of the Back Forest, which haunted the vicinity of Ludchurch, and terrified the benighted traveller as he wound along through the trees towards Castle Cliff, originated, I presume, like the far-famed "*Bosley Boggart,*" partly in the screams of an owl, partly in the roar of the winds along the forest glens, and partly in the half-sleeping mind of some simple cottager. To a like source also, coupled with the romantic character of the district, may be attributed the tales of terror which have found their way into so many mouths; and which find such willing auditors in the trippers and tourists who come hither from afar. Indeed, every little incident dimly shining in the far off past is made the foundation of a legend. A ghost is domiciled in every dark glen, and a tale told of every remarkable object. It is no wonder, therefore, that faint and obscure scraps of past history, which have been floating for years in the minds of the people, should come forth in new shapes and fantastic clothing when they are told in words. Still there are here many legends founded on truth; many from which some interesting fact may be obtained; yet it is not for me alone, but for every one to make his own selection of those he deems creditable, and, looking at their drift rather than their words, to deduce some new truth, or to dispel some dark old fiction by the light which they afford when opened.

7

Moorland superstitions

ONE of the most genuine relics of the olden time to be found in a district, seem to be its superstitions. In them we can trace the lingering effects of ancient, and now exploded notions; and from them form, combined with history and topography, a tolerably correct idea of, not merely how our ruder forefathers lived and acted, but also how they thought; and, to some extent, what they believed and felt.

Traditional Superstitions - and there seem to be no other sorts - appear to afford us glimpses into that inner feeling, under the current, as it were, of our ancestors' outward selves - of which we could gain no idea from anything else that has come down to us.

I have here given at random a number of those which, from many individual sources I have gathered in the Moorlands, without regard as to whether they are found elsewhere or not.

Beginning with those superstitions which seem connected with the religion of our forefathers, I may notice here a decided relic of the old worship and regard for the *Cross,* existing among a class Protestant to the back bone. The housewife crosses the witch out of her dough when she has kneaded it. The farmer (in some cases) puts a little wooden cross up in his cowhouse, above the heads of the in-calf cattle, to stop them from "picking" their calves before their time. The dairymaid, busy with her churn, will always cross her handful of salt ere she casts it in to alter the temperature. And if the butter do not form in reasonable time, she sometimes seeks a place in the floor where four flags meeting, leave a cross-shaped nick between them; and she will tell you, when the churn is put there, the butter soon comes.

Another way of conjuring butter has less to do with sacred symbols. Place the churn full of cream ready on retiring to bed, hang a new shirt over it, and leave the door slightly ajar. Next morning the shirt will be gone; and, thanks to the good fairy who fetched it, the butter churned. The belief in *fairies,* by the way, still lingers with some here, and in *witches* with many. A horseshoe may often be seen nailed to a stable-door to keep the witch out, and one or two persons believing themselves bewitched, have tramped long miles before breakfast to drink of the coloured water mentioned in an earlier part of these notes, and been cured. But some time ago the belief in witchcraft was much more prevalent. The hard clay floor of an old farmhouse in Leekfrith being dug up some time ago, an inverted glass bottle with a long neck, was found buried, full of a dark water, in which were about nine pins curiously bent. The worthy farmer supposed this was a charm for witchcraft - "One of his ancestresses had once been bewitched," he said, "and only broke the spell by catching the witch, and *drawing blood from her.*"

A protest against our finite knowledge, a yearning after the "hidden things" seems to be the very root and basis of many superstitions, as I think may appear from the following. Sometimes a bird will fly with force against the window pane - this is believed to be the herald of a message; or, boldly hopping into the house, it will tell its tidings in loud chirrups - "There will be news!" say the Moorlanders, and soon it is supposed to arrive. Or perhaps in an evening, when all are sitting round the table, a bit of wick will fall into the tallow of the candle, and lie flaming away too low - this is a "a thief," and so they look to their doors. Or a bright speck will appear in the candleflame; the young folk spy it, and cry "A Letter!" Or if a part of the tallow rolls over the side of the candle, it is a "winding sheet," and is received as a presage of death. Or perhaps when at breakfast a tiny sheet of smut will be seen hanging from a bar of the grate. This is "a stranger," and if he be not welcome they will clear off his herald with the poker.

Actions prognosticating ill-luck, or causing it, are very numerous here. To spill salt, to cut one's nails on a Friday, to see the new moon for the first time through glass, to turn again after once starting, to burn green elder wood, to have a string of birds' eggs in the house, &c., &c., are omens of ill. If the rustic's "nose itches he will be vexed," if his feet, he will "walk over strange ground;" if he "ties his stockings up in his garters he will be a wanderer and poor;" "if his left eye itches he will cry;" if his right he will laugh; "if his left ear burns hot some one is slandering him;"[9] nevertheless,

"Left or right is good at night."

Some superstitions seem to have more hold on the people than others. There are perhaps few Moorlanders to whom the above events would not convey the ideas here attached to them, and there are some who would be filled with real alarm if they heard the spider ticking his "death-watch", or saw a white cricket, or found a cinder like a coffin, or saw a solitary magpie fly over them, or heard a dog howl in the night, or broke a looking-glass, or heard a *token* (i.e. the lifting of an article, or hearing a sound they could not account for), for all these are the signs of death. And if in dreams they mingle with lost friends, or handle flesh meat, or pluck ripe fruit or see muddy water - then they would look out for trouble.

On the other hand: if a young man has a space between his front teeth sufficient for the insertion of a half-crown, or possesses hairy limbs, he will some day be "rich." "If you have money in your pocket when you first hear the cuckoo, you will have plenty all the year." If two magpies fly over 'tis a sign of a wedding; and, on a bridal day -
"Happy is the bride that the sun shines on."
If the sun shines through the fruit-trees on Christmas-Day it will be a good fruit year. If you find a horseshoe, or old nails, pocket them, 'tis good luck. If you see a certain sort of spider, pocket that too, if you can catch it, it is a "money spider."

But besides the general kind of omens, there are others, more like auguries. Perhaps, however, it must be confessed they are generally used only by the youthful fair sex, in order to ascertain a certain individual, and perhaps to hasten a certain day. An old dame confessed to me that when young she once went out into the garden with one or two companions, just before twelve o'clock one night, to discover "whom they were to have." As the clock struck they were plucking, in great fear, a leaf of sage at every stroke - when, lo! over the hedge he, who was afterwards my informant's husband, came leaping with a great scythe !!

Another way called "watching the supper," also used to be practised south of Buxton. There is to be a supper placed before the kitchen fire, and a free course left through the house. The girl is to sit watching this supper, when suddenly, if all be right, her future husband will rush in, take the supper, and instantly disappear - no questions are to be asked of him.

Turning from marriage beliefs to a less pleasant subject, much might be said on superstitions connected with the dead. Sometimes a figure of a person on the verge of decease is said to appear to friends. Tokens, too, indicating death are quite believed in; and if, when one sees a dead body one does not touch it, one shall dream of it. Tales, too, also are told of the spirit's re-appearance after death. A young man was buried in the churchyard at Rushton, with his feet to the West, in order too stop him from re-appearing. At Flash a house is said to have been taken down because it was haunted. But perhaps the following story, not as yet hinted at in these pages, will show all the popular points of belief in Moorland "ghosts." Mrs - living in the last century, not many miles from Leek, one day sent her maid to the well for water. The girl, by being long away, enraged her mistress so much that she thrashed her till - perhaps accidentally — she killed her. Of course there was a trial, but two things conspired to save the unlucky woman from the gallows; one was a "peck of guineas;" the other was this - she was being led to either the dead girl's body or heart, I forget which, in order that her guilt or innocence might be shewn by its bleeding or not at her touch. But on the way she asked leave to beg a cup of water, and this being granted the "law was thus broken and they could take her no further." Yet though she escaped the hand of justice, the good folk declare she had no peace. Every night the ghost of the poor girl haunted her bedside, and would never let her sleep before the cock crew in the morning. She was consequently obliged to get whom she could to stay up with her during the night. Sometimes two or three quarrelsome fellows would come in one night to sit within her, on account of the beer she dispensed; and tales are told of more than one fight happening in her house. At last affairs became so intolerable, that a number of clergy, twelve, I think, were gathered to "lay" the ghost. I do not know whether "Latin" was required to scare it away, but the story says they had "a rough time" of it. However, notwithstanding the fainting of one or two, some one or other of them read away till it was quietly laid on the Cloud-hillside, and afterwards it appeared only as a "phantom"[10] - a dim blue light often pointed out by the coachmen to night travellers.

Footnotes

(1)   Moorland word for a long piece of wood which fits into the heads of hammers, axes &c., and by which they are lifted and used. Pronounced stail amongst the more polite.

(2)   Stail, i.e. the handle or shaft of the hammer.

(3)   Soon after the Scottish rebellion, one James Shatwell built a hut in a deep dell, and it was called Hawk's-nest. He was a peculiar sort of person, and possessed a pair of bag-pipies. "He fetched his wife from Cannock." His dialect was somewhat strange o the inhabitants, with whom he had little to do,excepting the occasional trial of strength; and he occasionally left home, going no one knew whither. Some thought him a "Scotch rebel," who was hiding there; but he is said to have come from Hollingsclough, about five miles away.

(4)   This pit is one of considerable age. Round balls of some heavy metal have been found embedded in the coal, which turn out to be a mixture of iron and sulphur in small quantities. The farmers consider the coal found here to be of superior quality. If so, Mr Hand, the spirited lessee, deserves praise for the way in which he has pushed on his efforts, with no small skill, through many discouraging hindrances.

    No great distance from the mouth of this pit, old trees have been dug out of the ground by the farmers,in so sound a condition as to form good beams for roofing purposes.

(5)   Plott, and an old History now before me, mention this dyeing in the "alum water" before noted. "It dyes the button moulds black in half-an-hour's time, especially if they are made of oak; and with the least infusion of galls turns as black as ink." An old button maker told me that the moulds were dyed so as to prevent their colour showing much through the cloth with which they were to be covered. But it seems that they were first-dipped in water and then dried, so as to make the moulds shrink, and thus require less cloth to cover them. Thus the ingenious makers obtained a perquisite, since they had a certain quantity of cloth allowed for a definite number of buttons.

(6)   I follow the information I received from a former button maker, near Pannier's Pool.

(7)   The household secret purse of a Moorland family. The family hoard.

(8)   Roguish customs practised here from time immemorial.

(9)   The very words of the kind of proverb in which these superstitions are generally told. There are no doubt many others in the Moorlands than those I have quoted above, but as they are coy and only to be discovered by many occasional circumstances, I leave them for the research of more fortunate gatherers.

(10)   Of course I am now confining myself strictly to Moorland parlance. A ghost in the popular idea, when laid, became a phantom. This laying was rather a curious fact connected with ghosts, and was performed on several in this part of the county. Some of the names, as "Skag" attaching to some of them, especially the one at Bosley, alluded to in the note on Ludchurch and Flash; "Boggart" to all, "tuggin" &c., seem peculiar words - perhaps original as the myths to which they are attached.

APPENDIX 2

On 21 July 1881, seven years after the publication of 'Swythamley', about eighty members of the North Staffordshire Naturalist's Field Club, led by Thomas Wardle, visited the Wildboarclough vicinity. The following extract is taken from the Report and Proceedings of the Manchester Field-Naturalists and Archaeologists Society for that year.

Descending then the beautiful valley of the Dane, the party proceeded to Ludchurch, in the Leek Forest, an enormous crevice in the millstone grit rock, 208 ft. long, and about 40 ft. deep. Of this extraordinary place there is much legendary and traditional lore, and the sides of the crevice so overhang that snow has been known to remain through the summer. This is also supposed to have been one of the favourite haunts of the "headless rider," of whom even now strange tales are whispered. Leaving this uncanny "church" the party made a rapid march to Swythamley, the beautiful home of Mr Philip L. Brocklehurst, who had kindly given permission of inspection. The lovely grounds were fully explored, and the contents of the Hall examined, the latter affording a rich treat. Curiosities from all lands and of all ages, rare weapons of warfare and the chase, quaint pictures and engravings, and local relics abounded, and these were specially labelled by Mr Brocklehurst, this thoughtful attention adding materially to the pleasure of the visit. After tea, which was provided in a spacious room at the hall, the election and nomination of new members was proceeded with, and Mr W. CHALLINOR moved a vote of thanks to Mr Brocklehurst, who unfortunately was unable to be present, for allowing them to inspect his beautiful house and grounds, his curiosities and relics. - Dr ARLIDGE seconded the motion, regretting that they had not had more time to spend at Swythamley, The vote was carried by acclamation, and the party dispersed, having spent an exceedingly pleasant day.

IN STAFFORDSHIRE.

PARTICULARS

AND

CONDITIONS OF SALE

OF THE

ELEGANT MANSION HOUSE,

CALLED

SWITHAMLEY PARK

WITH THE PARK, MANOR,

AND SUNDRY VALUABLE

TITHE-FREE ESTATES,

SURROUNDING THE SAME,

Eligibly situated in the Townships of Heaton, Leek Frith, Tittesworth, in the County of Stafford,

CONTAINING

About 3,000 *Acres,*

WHICH

WILL BE SOLD BY AUCTION,

BY CLIFFE AND SON,

AT ST. ANN'S HOTEL, IN BUXTON,

IN THE COUNTY OF DERBY,

On Wednesday, the 10th of August, 1831.

AT TWO O'CLOCK IN THE AFTERNOON.

Cruso.

BROCKLEHURST & BAGSHAW,

Solicitors, Macclesfield.

J. SWINNERTON, PRINTER, MACCLESFIELD.

IN STAFFORDSHIRE.

Particulars and Conditions of Sale

OF THE

ELEGANT MANSION HOUSE,

CALLED

SWITHAMLEY PARK,

WITH THE PARK, MANOR,

AND SUNDRY VALUABLE

TITHE-FREE ESTATES,

SURROUNDING THE SAME,

MOST ELIGIBLY SITUATED IN THE TOWNSHIPS OF HEATON, LEEK-FRITH, AND TITTESWORTH,

IN THE COUNTY OF STAFFORD,

WITHIN EIGHT MILES OF BUXTON, SIX OF LEEK, SEVEN OF MACCLESFIELD,

And at a convenient distance from Manchester, comprehending in the whole

ABOUT 3,000 ACRES,

WHICH

WILL BE SOLD BY AUCTION,

BY MESSRS. CLIFFE AND SON,

AT SAINT ANN'S HOTEL, AT BUXTON,

IN THE COUNTY OF DERBY,

On Wednesday, the Tenth day of August, 1831,

AT TWO O'CLOCK IN THE AFTERNOON,

IN ONE LOT.

A proper Person will be appointed to shew the Property, and Particulars, and an ample Description thereof, may be had Twenty-eight days prior to the Sale, from Messrs. WALKER and JESSE, Solicitors, Manchester; GEORGE VERNON, Esq., Solicitor, Stone, in the County of Stafford; Mr. HEATON, Land Surveyor, Endon, near Leek; or at the Offices of Messrs. BROCKLEHURST and BAGSHAW, Solicitors, Macclesfield, where a Map of the Estates lies, and where further information may be obtained.

SWITHAMLEY MANSION

Has been recently erected of Stone, in the most beautiful part of the Park ; is as comfortable as it is convenient and spacious, having on the Ground Floor a Library, Breakfast Room, a Dining Room, and a Drawing Room.

The Doors are Mahogany, and the Drawing and Dining Rooms communicate by large Mahogany Folding Doors. On the same range there is a very large Kitchen, Servants' Hall, and in short every necessary convenience to so important a House.

The Stairs are of Stone, and the Hall paved with Hopton Stone ; a number of capital Bed Rooms, with Dressing Rooms ; and the Cellars are extensive and of the best temperature.

The Out-Offices form a square, and were built of Stone at the same time the House was erected, and contain Stables and Boxes for Twelve Horses, with Harness Room, Coach Houses, Dog Kennels, Coal Houses, and other convenient Buildings.

The Gardens and Pleasure Grounds are large and convenient, and suitable to such a Mansion.

The Park contains about Eighty Acres, is Walled round, and is well stocked with Deer ; is most excellent Land, and the Woods and Plantations in and about it, and the large Old Trees that seem almost to conceal the Ground, form one of the most picturesque and beautiful places in the Kingdom.

The Woods, which are considerable, are full of very fine Oak, Ash, and Alder Trees, ready to fall ; and an ample supply of Young Growing Trees remain to fill up the Woods, and many thousand Young Trees which have been planted on the Hills are in a very thriving state.

The Estate abounds with Game of every description, including Black Game.

The Hills afford excellent Grouse Shooting, and the Woods are notorious for the early appearance of Woodcocks, which may be found there in numbers at any time of the Season.

The Estate, with the exception of one or two small Farms, is in a Ring Fence, and is surrounded on the North and East sides by the Grouse Hills ; and the Mansion is nearly embosomed in a Wood of ancient Oaks, which are the resort of large quantities of Rooks.

There are two extensive Sheets of Water, and two smaller ones, on the Estate, which abound with fine Fish, and are frequented by Wild Fowl at the usual Seasons of the year.

The River Dane, celebrated for its high flavoured Trout, flows past the Boundary of part of the Property, the distance of five miles, and affords excellent sport for the Angler.

The fact that the Estate is not only totally exempt from Tithe, but that it is not even subject to a Modus, and that all other Rates affecting it are moderate, must be a strong inducement to possess such a Property.

It remains to be remarked that the Farm Houses and Buildings are in very good repair, the Agricultural Lands are well adapted for Farming purposes—that the Farms are all occupied by respectable Tenants ; and the Property, whether looked to as an Investment, as a Sporting Situation, or as the Residence of a Gentleman, an admirer of grand and beautiful Scenery, is one of the most desirable that can possibly be offered to the Public.

A SUMMARY OF THE ESTATE.

Names of the Tenants.	Description of the Premises.	Heaton.			Leek Frith.			Total.			Annual Value.		
		A.	R.	P.	A.	R.	F.	A.	R.	F.	£.	s.	D.
E. T. Trafford, Esq....	Swithamley Hall, Park, and other Farming Lands	102	3	3	...	...	...	102	3	3	245	15	11
Ditto	High Forest, or Back Forest, Roaches, and Gun...	...	...	...	469	2	13	469	2	13	70	12	11
Ditto	Woods, Plantations, and Pool.................	58	2	36	15	0	39	73	3	35	55	9	6
Ditto	Common Land, near Fairboroughs, not inclosed...	3	2	37	...	...	...	3	2	37	1	6	1
											Annual Rents.		
Joseph Armett........	Turner's Pool.. ..	...	...	...	29	1	17	29	1	17	36	0	0
Thomas Buxton........	High Forest	...	...	...	184	2	37	184	2	37	157	0	0
John Bosson	Hilly Lees	104	3	3	...	...	...	104	3	3	200	0	0
Isaac Bailey............	Old Smithys	56	3	35	...	...	...	56	3	35	70	0	0
William Brocklehurst	Dane Bridge	6	1	39	...	...	...	6	1	39	10	0	0
Joseph Belfield........	Springs Cottage	...	...	...	9	1	17	9	1	17	20	0	0
William Bestwick.....	Pool...	...	...	...	57	1	9	57	1	9	65	0	0
James Bestwick	Blackshaw Moor	...	...	...	19	2	36	19	2	36	15	15	0
Daniel Boyer	Whiteshaw Bottom.....	...	...	...	9	3	31	9	3	31	6	15	0
William Boyer........	Roaches	...	...	...	3	2	35	3	2	35	1	14	10
Thomas Clowes	Paddock...	12	2	2	41	3	22	54	1	24	70	0	0
Ellen Corden............	Dane Bridge	10	1	15	...	...	...	10	1	15	16	0	0
William Cooper	Meadows..	...	...	...	76	1	15	76	1	15	100	0	0
James Earlham.........	Dane Bridge	1	2	38	...	...	...	1	2	38	16	0	0
Thomas Goodwin	Shaw Bank	2	1	35	...	...	...	2	1	35	6	0	0
John Goodwin	Roaches	...	...	...	622	1	6	622	1	6	15	0	0
James Gould............	Roaches	...	...	...	37	2	37	37	2	37	25	5	0
Joshua Heapy	Gun	82	3	12	...	...	...	82	3	12	18	18	0
Edward Heapy........	Beardhall Mill	74	0	28	...	...	...	74	0	28	144	0	0
James Hunt	Dane Bridge	3	2	18	...	...	...	3	2	18	8	10	0
John Hunt	High Ridge..	...	...	...	35	0	28	35	0	28	40	0	0
Edward Hassall	Pheasant Clough	...	...	..	173	1	21	173	1	21	130	0	0
John Mellor	Roster	...	...	...	48	3	22	48	3	22	50	0	0
Matthew Mellor	Springs...	...	...	...	60	0	1	60	0	1	60	0	0
Joseph Mills	Clough Head	...	...	..	71	3	19	71	3	19	52	10	0
Thomas Mason	Browns Piece..	...	...	...	85	1	24	85	1	24	30	0	0
John Nadin	Bent End	41	1	37	...	...	...	41	1	37	50	0	0
Isaac Poyser............	Dane Wood	76	1	17	...	...	...	76	1	17	27	10	0
Thomas Pickford	Shaw	...	...	...	12	1	19	12	1	19	8	0	0
William Slack	Hanging Stone	174	3	4	...	...	...	174	3	4	115	0	0
James Shaw	....	23	3	6	...	...	...	23	3	6	36	0	0
David Sheldon	Blackshaw Moor, in Tittesworth.................... ..	...	...	...	21	0	16	21	0	16	15	15	0
Joseph Turnock	Withy Stakes	...	...	...	26	2	34	26	2	34	39	0	0
Robert Turnock	Roaches	...	...	...	6	2	2	6	2	2	3	10	0
Workhouse	....	0	0	4	...	...	...	0	0	4	8	0	0
	Grand Total................	837	2	9	2118	2	20	2956	0	29	2040	7	2

For your notes .....

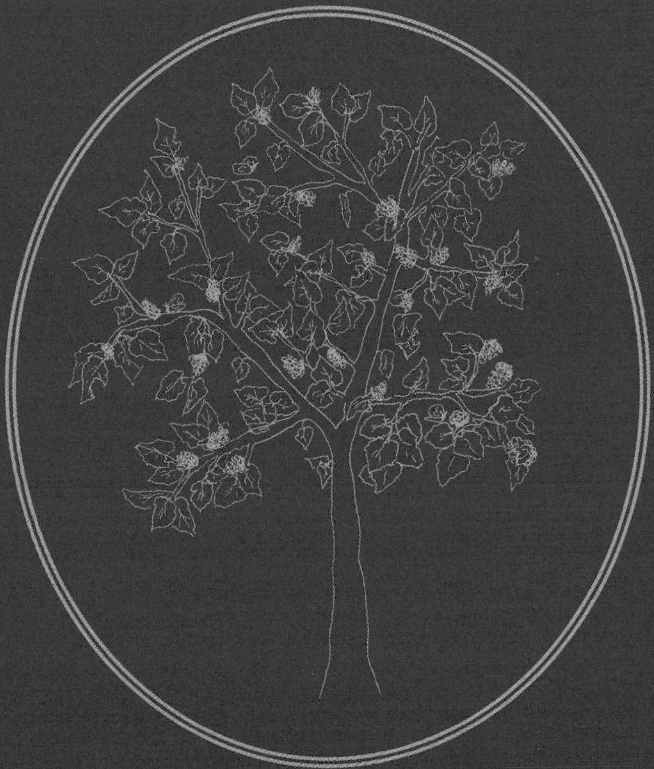